SILVERSMITH OF OLD NEW YORK:
Myer Myers

BOOKS BY WILLIAM WISE

JONATHAN BLAKE
The Life and Times of a Very Young Man

SILVERSMITH OF OLD NEW YORK
Myer Myers

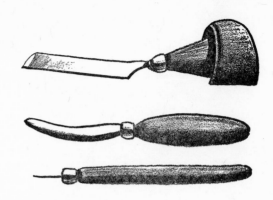

Silversmith
of Old New York:
Myer Myers

BY WILLIAM WISE

Illustrated by Leonard Everett Fisher

Farrar, Straus and Cudahy

Jewish Publication Society

Contents

AUTHOR'S NOTE

For the sake of complete accuracy, it should be pointed out that Myer Myers was both a goldsmith and a silversmith (a common practice of the craft in the 18th century) and that to avoid confusing the younger reader I have referred to him only as the latter in this biography. In addition, while no record of the Isaac Seixas Menorah exists today, the making of such a piece was well within the talents of the young apprentice, and the commissioning of it would in no way have been unusual for a man of Isaac Seixas' position.

Three books were of particular help in the writing of this biography. The first, *Myer Myers, Goldsmith,* by Jeannette W. Rosenbaum (The Jewish Publication Society of America), provided a wealth of careful documentation about the subject's life. *Social New York Under the Georges,* by Esther Singleton (D. Appleton & Co.), and *Silver* by Gerald Taylor (Penguin Books Ltd.), proved almost equally useful.

PART ONE

THE EARLY YEARS

1. *"What Shall I Become?"*

One summer afternoon, in the year 1736, a man and a boy appeared together at the foot of one of the wooden wharves in New York City. Except for the two of them, the place was deserted. The man looked around, and then sat down on an empty crate, and the boy sat down beside him.

The man's name was Solomon Myers. He was a shopkeeper in the city, though he wasn't a very successful one. He looked at the boy for a moment, and then he said, "Myer, I want to have a talk with you. A very important talk."

Myer Myers was the oldest son of Solomon and Judith Myers, two of the earliest Jewish settlers in the colony of New York. He was thirteen years old that summer afternoon, and like any other boy his age, he could have thought of a dozen things he would rather have been doing instead of sitting next to his father waiting for a "lecture" of some kind.

Myer's father didn't say anything for awhile. The longer he was silent the more certain Myer felt that this was to be no ordinary lecture. He began to wonder if he'd done anything especially bad lately. But as far as he could remember he hadn't been in any more mischief than usual, so he didn't see how it could be that. He turned his clear, gray eyes on his father and began to wonder what it was all about.

Solomon Myers finally put his hands on his knees and turned to look at his son. "I want to talk to you about the future," he said. "*Your* future, Myer. You won't be a child much longer. Soon you'll have to decide what you want to make of your life."

Myer nodded his head slowly. This *was* important. His father had never talked to him like this before—almost as though they were equals instead of a father talking to his oldest son.

"Now it isn't something you have to decide today," his father went on. "I want you to finish your schooling first. I want you to get as much education as you can, because there's almost nothing as important to a man's happiness as the knowledge he can get from reading and study. So, for another two or three years, you'll go on with your lessons and help me in the shop, just the way you've always done."

Myer nodded again.

"But in the meantime," his father said, "I want you to be thinking about it, so that when the time comes you'll make a wise choice. Whatever you decide on, it will be the work you'll do for the rest of your life. So—it isn't a choice to be made lightly."

"I'm sure that it isn't," Myer said.

He was also very sure of something else, but he didn't say anything about the thought that crossed his mind just then. All the same, he knew that his father was being exceptionally kind and generous to him in allowing him to choose his own vocation. Many fathers in the city told their sons what they were going to be, and that was that. Many fathers forced their sons to go into the same work that they were in themselves. Or else, if they had a number of sons, they apprenticed them, one by one, to whatever kind of work happened to be open at the time.

Myer would have liked to thank his father, but he didn't know how. So he sat on the side of the wharf and looked at the calm blue water of the bay and the trees on the nearby shore of Long Island and listened while his father spoke again.

"Of course, you could stay with me in our shop," Solomon Myers said. "You know something about it already. I'd be pleased to have you stay, and when you're older you could help me to run the shop as my partner."

Solomon Myers sighed, and then he said, "But on the other hand, you might be fitted for something else. *I* haven't done very well as a shopkeeper, and for all I know maybe you aren't cut out to be one either."

Myer had never heard his father talk like this before. He knew, of course, that his father's shop was not as successful as it might have been; several years before, his father had been forced to find extra work to support his family. The synagogue had hired him to look after the building and the grounds, and for this he was paid a salary in money and goods— eight cords of wood each year for himself and his family, to warm the house on Stone Street where they lived.

Myer had never seen his father look quite as sad as he looked at that moment on the wharf, as they talked about his unsuccessful business. But Solomon Myers didn't stay sad for long. He seemed to throw back his shoulders and take in a breath of fresh air, and then a smile broke out on his face.

He was himself again. Even his voice sounded more light-hearted and natural. "So —there we are, Myer," he said. "Now you understand why I told you to come for a walk with me today. In the next few months you want to start thinking about your future. Or maybe you've got some ideas already?"

"I haven't made up my mind yet," Myer

said gravely. "But I'll think about it. I certainly will. Maybe I'll become a . . . no, I'd better think some more about it first."

"That's right, you consider it carefully," his father said. And then they both got up and left the wharf and slowly walked back together to the house on Stone Street.

For weeks and weeks there was little else that Myer Myers thought about. Whenever he was free he walked from one side of the town to the other and watched different men at work and tried to decide which job was the right one for him.

He knew, of course, without his father telling him, that there were certain things he couldn't hope to become. Had he lived in our own day, things would have been different. But in 1736 most boys didn't go to college, so they couldn't become doctors or lawyers or architects.

There were only three or four colleges in all the thirteen colonies in those days, and their enrollment was very small and the cost of attending them very high. Most children stayed in a local school as long as they could—often not more than six or seven years—and then, especially if their parents were poor, they went to work.

For Jewish boys like Myer Myers there were two principal ways to earn a living. They could go into trade, the way Solomon Myers had done, or they could become indentured and serve seven years as an apprentice to a craft worker before setting up in business for themselves. If they became apprenticed, it might be to a harness maker, where they would learn to work with leather goods. Or it might be to a wheelwright, where they would learn to make wheels for the new carriages that were beginning to appear in the city, or for the farmers' wagons that carried the grain to market. Or it might be to a cooper, where they would learn to make the stout barrels that carried the rum and sugar on the ships plying back and forth between the West Indies and New York.

At first Myer thought it might be better to stay with his father and become a shopkeeper instead of becoming an apprentice and learning a craft. His father's shop was on the ground floor of their house on Stone Street. Since he was a small boy Myer had worked there, and he knew where the stock was kept, how to show samples to the customers and how to mark the amount of each sale in his father's account book. He liked to work in the store well enough—unless he could find an excuse for getting outside and playing with the boys who lived in the neighborhood. Then he quickly forgot the shop—until he heard his father or his mother calling him back to work again.

But now, the more he thought about it the more he began to wonder if he really wanted to become a shopkeeper after all. Working in the shop was all right when there wasn't anything better to do. But sometimes, especially in the summer when he had to mind the shop all afternoon, the hours seemed to drag on forever. Hardly any customers came in. Sometimes there was no one to talk to for hours at a time, except his mother and father. His younger brother, Asher, would be outside playing, or watching the other children—Joseph or the girls, Slowey Sarah or Rebecca, who was still a baby.

The place was hot, his eyes would slide shut, he would almost be asleep, when his father would come in and shake him by the shoulder. "Here, Myer, is this how you watch the shop when I'm gone for a moment?" And Myer would sit up and rub his eyes and try to keep awake. And finally his father would tell him to run outside and play with the others because he didn't need him inside any longer.

No—the more Myer thought of it now the more he felt that he didn't really want to stay with his father and be a shopkeeper. As much as he loved his father and as much as he liked to be with him, there was really nothing about running the shop that interested him.

Maybe, he began to realize, he didn't want to be a merchant or a trader at all. So one afternoon he went down to the wharves on the East River and watched what the merchants did when they gathered there to inspect the cargoes coming in on the ships.

It was an exciting moment when one of the ships arrived. The wharves would be crowded with sailors, men with untidy beards and sunburned faces who had been at sea for as long as three or four months. They would swagger down the wharves or lean over the gunwhales of their ships and shout to the friends they spied on shore. Or else they'd come striding down the wharf to unload the bales and barrels from the ships, jingling coins in their pockets as they moved about and singing snatches of music that was like no other music in the world.

Myer watched the sailors that afternoon—and forgot completely about being a shop-keeper. It was clear that being a sailor was the best thing in the world to be. You lived in the open, on the rolling sea, and never had to wait for customers to come in and buy the goods in your store. You were a free man. And at the end of a voyage you returned to port with nothing but gold and silver in your pockets.

When the afternoon was over he ran all the way back to the house and burst into the kitchen, where his mother was cooking supper.

"I've made up my mind!" he shouted. "I know what I'm going to be!"

Judith Myers looked up from the pot she was stirring. "You've decided already?" she said. "Well—what is it then?"

"I'm going to be a sailor," he said. "I just saw some sailors unloading a ship down at Murray's Wharf. I'm going off to sea as soon as I'm old enough. I'll visit all the places I've read about. I'll see everything there is to see, and then I'll come back home with a lot of gold and silver to spend as I please."

Judith Myers began to laugh as she stirred the pot. And when Myer saw that she was laughing he grew angry, for he was a boy with a quick temper.

"Well, why *shouldn't* I become a sailor?" he said. "What are you laughing at me for? I guess I can become a sailor if I feel like it."

His mother looked down at Myer and put her hand on his head and ran her fingers through his dark hair. "I'm not laughing at you," she said. "I'm laughing because I remember what happened the day that you and some friends of yours tried to row across the river to Long Island. Remember what happened?"

Myer lowered his eyes and felt his cheeks burn. "I got seasick," he said.

His mother laughed again, but gently this time. "That's right—so what kind of a sailor would you make, if you get seasick so easily? And besides, if you become a sailor you'd never be home. You'd hardly ever see your father or me. You'd hardly ever see Asher or your sisters—is that the kind of life you want to live? Spending ten months out of every year on board a ship?"

"I hadn't thought of all that," Myer said.

His mother turned to the fire again. "Don't you see?" she said. "You have to think carefully before you choose your life work. Just because something *seems* to be exciting, that doesn't mean it really is when you have to do it day after day, year in and year out. And it doesn't mean that you, Myer, are really suited for it. You must be patient. And then one day, maybe when you least expect it, you'll discover what you were really meant to be. You'll *know* —because the idea of it will fill you with happiness."

Myer nodded slowly. Now that he really stopped to *think* about it, now that he wasn't completely carried away, the idea of becoming a sailor and spending his life on a ship wasn't nearly as exciting as it had seemed at first. There were other things to become. He had to think about it—and learn to make up his mind more carefully.

But in another week or two he'd already forgotten that he was going to think things out slowly. He wasn't that sort of person anyway. He liked to study a problem and then get it settled as quickly as possible. So before very long he made up his mind again.

This time he decided that he wanted to be a blacksmith. Like the man in the shop on Burnett Street, around the corner from the Meal Market. This time, he was sure, he had made the right choice.

His father and mother both shook their heads when they heard it. "But you don't even like horses!" Solomon Myers said. And he frowned, the way he always did when something was troubling him. "What kind of a boy are you, Myer? Where's the common sense that God should have given you? You don't like horses—so you want to be a blacksmith!"

Myer's mother was more patient, as she almost always was with the children. She said, "Tell us, Myer, what put the idea of being a blacksmith into your head?"

Myer frowned and tried to explain it. "I decided," he said, "when I passed the blacksmith's shop the other day and stopped to watch him. There was so much going on—not like here, in our shop, where nothing ever happens. There was the fire, and the way he kept blowing on it with his bellows, and then beating the shoes out with his hammer on the anvil, and the sparks flying, and everyone watching him make the shoes."

"Was there anything else you saw there?" his mother said, "that made you think you'd like to be a blacksmith?"

Myer's eyes grew bright for a moment. "Yes, there was," he finally said. "There was the part about his making the shoes—if a man is a blacksmith, then he can make something with his own hands. Something that wouldn't exist if it weren't for the work he was doing. That's why I'd like to be a blacksmith. So I can make something with my own hands instead of just buying and selling in the store."

His mother and father saw the excitement in his eyes, and Solomon Myers began to feel sorry for the way he'd lost his temper. "With your own hands," Solomon said. "Well, maybe there's some sense in it after all. Still, there's no hurry. Look around some more, Myer. And then we'll see if you change your mind or not."

Myer's father was right, as things turned out. Before long Myer went back to the blacksmith's shop again, only this time he seemed to see things in a different light.

A farmer had brought in his horse to be shod. The horse was frightened by the blacksmith's fire and by the noise of the hammer crashing down on the anvil.

While the blacksmith turned and blew on the fire with his bellows, the horse reared on its hind legs and tried to break away from the man who was holding him. The horse snorted and kicked the dirt in front of the shop till the ground shook.

By the time Myer came home for lunch that day he knew he had made another mistake by being too hasty. He said to his mother and father, with a sheepish smile, "I think I've changed my mind again. I may not want to be a blacksmith after all. I'd like to *make* things —but I'm not sure I want to make horseshoes."

Judith Myers put a bowl of steaming soup in front of him and told him not to worry about it. "You'll find out one day, when the time comes. And then you'll know what you were meant to be, the way I told you."

But it was the best part of summer now, and Myer was tired of thinking so much about serious things anyway. He wanted to have some fun for a change. So after lunch he slipped away with his brother, Asher, and quickly forgot all about his troubles as they walked along the streets of the town.

In those days New York was a wonderful

place to be, especially in the summertime. The
city itself was so different from what it is now
that such a change can hardly be imagined. It
was a very small town then, with only about
five thousand inhabitants. There were no sky-
scrapers, no buses, no subways or noise or confusion. All around, where some of the tallest
buildings in the world stand today, there were
trees and meadows, rivers and ponds, a few
farms and miles of rolling hills and untouched
woodlands. And to the south, at the extreme
end of Manhattan Island, there was the city itself, with its wharves, its pretty houses and its
narrow, old-fashioned streets.

Because it had the finest harbor in all the
colonies, New York was already growing into
the most important shipping center on the entire coast. Trading ships sailed from its docks
to England with raw materials and returned
with manufactured goods and with food and
rum picked up in the West Indies. The harbor
was always dotted with ships, and almost every
day one or more spread its sail, raised anchor
and made its way down the channel into the
Atlantic Ocean.

At the south end of the city Myer and his
brother stopped and watched one of the ships,

its sails open full to catch the wind, sailing across the harbor on its way to the sea. Then they began to walk on till at last they came to the Governor's Fort.

Here they could see the English soldiers in their bright uniforms, and here, beyond the high wall and the gate, stood a dozen cannon, pointing out across the harbor. And in the center of the fort there stood a house of red brick, where the most important man in the colony, the English governor, lived.

The governor's house was one of the handsomest houses in the city, but there were other houses almost as handsome that Myer and Asher passed as they began to walk away from the harbor. Some of them were also made of brick, especially the ones on Pearl Street, where the finest families lived, but most of the houses in the city were made of wood. They were neat and clean, and the streets in front of them were mostly paved and kept in good condition, for each householder was held responsible for keeping the section in front of his house in repair.

There were trees planted in front of the houses, beech trees for shade and locust trees that had sweet-smelling blossoms that filled the air with perfume on summer afternoons like this.

Before very long—because the city itself was less than a mile in length from the Governor's Fort to the last of the houses on the northern end—Myer and Asher found themselves walking through open meadows, past a scattering of farm houses and finally through the woods itself. They stopped and drank from a spring and then sprawled out under a shade tree and listened to the chattering of the birds and the whir of the insects all around them.

Myer had forgotten about serious matters by now. He and Asher found stones near the brook and threw them, trying to make the stones skip on top of the water. Then they took off their shoes and stockings and cooled their feet in the water of a little stream, and after awhile, tired from being outdoors and from walking and running so much, they came back home.

That night Myer had a new thought: he didn't want to become anything at all. Not a shopkeeper, nor a sailor, nor a blacksmith. He wanted to live just the way he had that afternoon, with no work to do, no troubles on his mind and Asher to keep him company. And

every day of his life he'd be perfectly free to
walk from one end of New York to the other,
to loaf and play games and to go to bed at
night so tired that he could hardly keep his
eyes open.

Only Myer didn't tell his father any of this.
He knew that his father was a good man and
worked hard to clothe and feed them all. Most
times his father understood things, and his
mother even more, but maybe his father
wouldn't remember what it was like to be a
boy of thirteen on a perfect summer afternoon, when you wanted to stay just the way
you were, forever.

Work is hard, Myer thought sleepily. I don't
want to be anything. And that was the last
thing he thought of before he fell asleep.

The summer passed slowly, and then most
of the autumn. But even though time was slipping by Myer found that he wasn't any closer
to making up his mind than he had been in
the beginning.

One week he was almost happy at the
thought of being apprenticed to a cooper—till
he decided that he'd soon get tired of making

nothing but barrels. Then he thought of becoming a harness maker—but why not a wheelwright instead? The next week he was ready
to become a brazier—a craftsman who worked
in bronze, making metal parts for houses and
farms and especially the roofs of important
buildings.

But even being a brazier wasn't *exactly* what
he wanted to become, and he began to wonder
if he'd ever find the one thing in the world
that would satisfy him for the rest of his life.
Or—if there really was such an occupation.

Myer had almost decided that it didn't make
any difference what he became, when one autumn day a customer who was in their shop
asked him if he would run an errand for him.
The customer was planning to pick up a pair
of candlesticks from the silversmith in the
next street, if the candlesticks were ready. He
asked Myer to go and learn what condition
they were in.

Myer ran down the street, turned the corner
and stopped at the door of the silversmith's
shop. He had never been inside a silversmith's
before. Families as poor as Solomon Myers'
had little reason to visit there. Only the rich
could afford to buy silver and gold and have

them fashioned into pitchers and teapots, tankards and spoons.

Myer pushed open the door and heard the tinkling of a bell overhead. He stepped inside —and seemed to enter another world. A world so bright and dazzling, so gleaming with reflected light, that his eyes felt blinded for a moment.

The silversmith was working near the fireplace. He was making a bowl, Myer remembered afterward, a silver bowl with a neatly fitted silver lid. It was the most beautiful thing that Myer Myers had ever seen.

To make something like that, Myer thought, would be wonderful. To be skilled enough to be able to work in silver for the rest of your life. To make things in silver as beautiful as that bowl.

A feeling had come over him different from any sensation he had ever known. And he remembered his mother's words: "When you discover what you were meant to be, you'll *know*—because the idea of it will fill you with happiness."

I shall become a silversmith, Myer said to himself. And this time, he knew he had made the right decision.

2. An Apprentice

At first Myer didn't tell his parents what had happened. He remembered how, a few months before, he had rushed home and said that he wanted to be a sailor, then a blacksmith, and how he had changed his mind not long afterward. This time he wanted to be absolutely sure he had made the right choice before he told anyone about it.

But he needn't have worried. As the weeks went by he found himself more eager than ever to become a silversmith. Nothing else interested him. The beauty of what he had seen in the silversmith's shop stayed fresh in his mind. He could only wonder how he had ever wanted to be anything else. A sailor?—ridiculous. A blacksmith?—ridiculous too. A brazier, or a wheelwright, or anything else *except* a silversmith? The thought almost made him tremble with unhappiness.

And then he began to worry about something else. Maybe his father and mother wouldn't let him do what he wanted. They might change their minds, and decide that they were a better judge of what trade he should follow than he was himself. Or there might be a diffent reason why he couldn't become a silversmith. A reason he didn't know anything about.

Could anyone in New York, he wondered, become a silversmith? Could an ordinary Jewish boy like himself? Or was there some kind of colonial law that decreed who could become a silversmith and who could not, and would that law prevent him from realizing his ambition?

Myer grew more and more afraid of telling his parents what he had decided. If they said it was impossible he couldn't imagine what he would do. So he hung back until the uncertainty became too much to bear.

Then one night after supper, when the other children, even Asher, were upstairs in bed, he said to his mother and father, "I know what I want to be. This time I'm sure of it."

His father had been adding and subtracting figures in his business account book. Whenever he looked at the book there was always a troubled frown on his face. Now the frown seemed to grow a little deeper.

"You've decided, Myer?" he said. "Well, what's it to be this time?"

Myer lowered his eyes and said very softly, "I would like to be apprenticed to a silversmith."

Myer saw his mother and father exchange a hurried glance, and then he heard his father sigh heavily. His mother said, "Tell us why you want to be a silversmith, Myer."

He told them as quickly as he could. He described what he had seen that day in the shop,

and how he had known, from the very first moment, that the one thing in life he wanted the
most was to make beautiful objects out of silver. He told them how he hadn't thought of
anything else ever since the day he'd been inside the shop.

Solomon Myers stood up and put the account book away on a shelf. After that he sat
down again and looked at his son.

"If that's what you really want," he said,
"then I'll do everything I can to see that you
have your chance. But I can't promise it for
sure, Myer. I just don't know. . . ."

Judith Myers said, "You see, there's the cost
of your being apprenticed, Myer. The truth is,
it's very expensive to apprentice a boy to a
silversmith. More expensive than to apprentice him to anyone else. You know your father
isn't a rich man—but if that's what you really
want, I know he'll do everything that he can
to make it possible."

"Yes, I will," Solomon Myers said. "But I
can't promise you for sure. . . ."

"Thank you," Myer said. "It *is* what I want
. . . and I'll always be grateful for the
chance. . . ."

Myer felt ashamed that he was causing his

parents more trouble than ever. But it *was* what he wanted—and somehow he knew it was the one thing he was meant to become. And he would pay them back for their effort, and for the hardship he was causing them. He swore that he would, and that night in bed he prayed to God to help him, so that he could return as much to his parents as he had received from them.

For three years Solomon and Judith Myers saved as much money as possible to pay the cost of apprenticing Myer to a silversmith. They realized that their eldest son would never be happy at any other work, but it wasn't easy for them to save money.

They had to do it a little bit at a time. Solomon gave up the idea of buying cloth to make a new suit for himself. Judith spent her few pennies for household expenses with extreme care, and together they put aside what they saved and added to the sum whenever they could. It was hard, but it was the only thing that poor people could do in those days when they wanted to help their children.

All the same, those three years were happy ones for the Myers family. The children were healthy and growing bigger and stronger each year. They all had enough to eat, enough clothes to wear and enough wood in the fireplace to keep the house warm.

Myer and the other children went to the little school that was run by the Synagogue of the Shearith Israel Congregation. In the colonies there was still no regular system of public education, and there wouldn't be any for a number of years to come. At the synagogue's school they learned Hebrew and English as well as Dutch and Spanish. Myer could read and speak all four languages fluently. And the things that he began to read about Holland and England and other places in Europe made him curious to learn how his parents had lived before they came to America.

Sometimes at night he and Asher sat up with their parents and asked them about life in the Old World. Their mother would look up from her sewing and their father would smile his happiest smile, and he would say to Myer and Asher, "Well, whatever it was like in Holland, it wasn't as good as life is now, here in New York."

Solomon Myers looked like an old man now, though he was only in his late thirties. The doctor said that he had a weak chest and had let his health run down. That's what made his face look gray sometimes and made him cough so much. But when he was talking like this to Myer and Asher, the years seemed to fall away and he became almost a young-looking man again.

"Yes, but what was Holland really like?" Myer would ask his father. "When did you first think of leaving there? And why? Asher and I heard a man and his wife talking the other day. They'd just gotten off the boat, and they said the trip across was terrible. When you and mother crossed was it terrible too?"

"It was, it was," their father told them. "We ran into a great storm. It lasted for two weeks. And for two weeks they kept all the passengers locked below the decks. It was terrible all right —but it was worth it, once we got here."

"Was life in Holland so different then?" Asher said.

"Completely," their father told them. "We lived with your mother's family, three families all together in one house. It wasn't a ghetto— we had no ghettos in Holland—but still, we lived like nothing you've ever seen here. All the Jews were restricted in what they could do to make a living. There were laws and more laws, restrictions and more restrictions. And Holland was almost the best country in Europe for the Jews. That was one of the reasons we first thought of crossing to America."

"But how did you know things would be better here?" Myer said.

"Yes, how could you be sure?" said Asher.

"We couldn't be," Solomon Myers said. "But we heard stories from people who were here in New York already. They told us that the English were very fair to people of *all* faiths. In England they were making reforms to free the Jews—we knew this, of course. But we heard that things were moving even more quickly here. People wrote and said that this was a new country. New ideas were growing here. People didn't care what your religion was. There was no persecution, the way there had been in Europe for a thousand years. We heard that people here didn't go in for such things. Many of them had fled religious persecution themselves. And they were too busy trying to make a place for themselves to have time to hate or be cruel to their fellow human beings."

Solomon shook his head, and his eyes shone bright as he recalled the days when he was a younger man. "Your mother and I had just been married a year," he said. "And we kept hearing about America, America, and how there was a new world, a whole new continent, where a man could come and be free—like he never could be free in Europe. Free to do what he wanted for a living, to think and worship as he pleased. We were young and strong, and we dreamed of such a world as America. So one day we took all the money we had and bought our passage to come here."

Judith Myers had forgotten her sewing now as she looked at her husband. He said to the boys, "What a day that was! Everyone crying to see us go—but we were happy all the same. Happy and scared. We knew we were going on the greatest adventure of our lives. And we knew it would be the most wonderful thing for ourselves and our children—or the most terrible. Isn't that right, Mother? Weren't we happy and scared, all at the same time?"

Myer's mother looked away at the fire. There were tears in her eyes, tears that came from thinking of all the things she had left behind in order to come to a new land with her husband.

"We were frightened," she said. "At least

I was. And the trip on the boat. Myer, you would have been so seasick. It's a good thing you weren't even born yet. I don't know what I would have done with you."

"And then," Solomon said, "we reached New York. Right away I could see things were different here. I set up my shop without any interference from the government. And the year you were born, Myer, that was the year that a new law was passed making all Jews in the colony free men. Citizens. That's when I knew for sure that your mother and I had been right in coming here to live and raise our family."

The room was dark now. The fire had almost burned itself out on the grate. Solomon's face was hidden by shadows, but Myer could still see his smile—he always remembered afterward the way his father had looked that night when he had told them about coming to America.

"This must be a wonderful country then," Myer said. He was a little surprised at the idea, for he had never thought much about the difference between Europe and America.

"It is," Solomon told him. "And it can become more and more wonderful, a better and better place to live, if the people here will work to make it so. There's nothing that ever gets done, Myer, without work."

"And no work that ever gets done without sleep," Judith said. She looked up at the fire and then at her two sons. Myer was still wide awake, but Asher, as usual, was dozing off.

"Now you two get up to bed," she told them. And Myer gave Asher a shake till he was awake and then they both left the fire and went upstairs to sleep, taking with them visions of the Old World and the New, and all of the adventures their parents had known in coming to America.

When three years had finally passed, and Myer was sixteen, his father decided it was time for him to begin his apprenticeship. Solomon and his wife talked the situation over. They had managed to save twenty-seven pounds. Neither of them knew for sure whether such a sum would be enough to pay for Myer, while he was learning his craft, so Solomon said to Judith, "I will take Myer and go and find out."

They set out one cold winter morning. Myer's father was bundled up in his heavy coat, and underneath he wore the same dark suit that he'd thought of replacing—the suit a little thinner in the knees now, and a little shinier in the seat of the trousers.

Myer walked at his side, tall and thin, an inch or two taller than his father. He was no longer a child, anyone could tell that. His face wore a serious expression. But inside his chest his heart was beating with excitement, for he believed this to be the most important day of his life.

Solomon and Myer first went to a man named Cornelius Kierstede, who was said to be the finest silversmith in New York. Solomon introduced himself and his son. He explained to the smith that he wanted to apprentice Myer, and that he naturally thought of Mr. Kierstede as the best craftsman he could place him with.

Then Myer was left by himself while the two men went inside Mr. Kierstede's parlor to discuss the matter. Myer used the chance to look at the pieces which the silversmith was working on. There were several newly finished objects: a teapot, waiting to be brought to a final polish, some spoons and forks—forks with only three prongs, the way they were made around that time—and a thin silver tray. Myer didn't touch them, but he examined them as closely as he could and began to understand why Mr. Kierstede was so highly respected in his craft.

The detail work on the teapot was done with extreme care. And even the salver, which was what a little tray like that was called, though plain in design, was beautifully made too.

Myer heard a noise behind him and saw his father and Mr. Kierstede emerge from the parlor. Solomon Myers' face wore a bewildered expression. Myer knew that he had met with failure, and his own heart sank. It didn't help to hear old Mr. Kierstede say, "But I'm sure you'll find someone else, Mr. Myers. I hope you understand. . . ."

Mr. Kierstede hadn't wanted an apprentice, Solomon told Myer once they were back in the street. And even if he had—the cost for apprenticing a boy with him would be at least fifty pounds. . . .

"We must try somewhere else," his father said with a sigh.

There were two other silversmiths who were well known in New York, and Myer and his father went to their shops after their visit to Mr. Kierstede. The first man was Benjamin Wynkoop, who said he would accept Myer as an apprentice—for fifty pounds. And the other was Pieter Van Dyck, whose shop Myer had been inside three years before. Mr. Van Dyck wanted just as much as the others, in fact a few pounds more. At both shops Solomon Myers smiled, said he would think it over and then left with Myer at his heels. He didn't admit that he didn't have the money, but in each place he pretended that there were other considerations that were holding him back from apprenticing his son then and there.

It was almost noon by the time they returned to the house on Stone Street. The world had never seemed so dark to Myer. He was too upset to notice, and too young to understand, that his mother and father felt worse than he did. They needed another twenty-three pounds for their son—and they didn't have any way of getting it.

They ate lunch in silence. It was the longest lunch Myer could remember eating. And he didn't eat much of it. His mind could think of only one thing—I'm not going to be able to be a silversmith after all. Because we are poor people. . . . I shall never be able to spend my life making beautiful things out of silver. Because we're too poor. . . .

But Solomon Myers wasn't defeated so easily. He pushed back his chair and told Judith and Myer, "I have a new idea. At first I thought I should go to the best silversmiths, because I wanted Myer to have a chance to learn his trade with only the best. But now I think I made a mistake. Suppose it's a question of learning with someone who isn't quite so good—or not learning at all?"

"Do you know another silversmith?" Judith said.

"I do," Solomon told them. "A man named Wilhelm Skatts. Do you remember? He was in our shop last summer."

Judith frowned. "The one who never paid his account?"

Solomon nodded. "I told you he wasn't the sort of man I'd pick out *first,* but now what other choice is there? He doesn't always pay his debts on time because his business isn't so good. As a matter of fact, I've heard people say that the things he makes aren't always so good either. He's not in a class with Mr. Van Dyck or Mr. Wynkoop or Mr. Kierstede. *But,* if he needs money, maybe he's the man who will teach our Myer at a price we can afford to pay."

It seemed like a good plan, especially since there wasn't any other plan they could think of. So that afternoon Solomon and Myer set off again, this time to the shop of Wilhelm Skatts.

Mr. Skatts lived several blocks away, on Dock Street, not far from the East River. His shop was on the ground floor of a dark, ill-painted frame house, a house that was dark with dirt if you looked closely.

Mr. Skatts looked a bit dirty too. He had dark, oily hair, and the collar and cuffs of his shirt were dirty around the edges. He was a man about Solomon's age, but almost half a head taller. He had a barrel chest and huge arms, and Myer couldn't help but think that someone with so much muscular strength might have made a better carpenter or a black-smith.

At first Mr. Skatts eyed them suspiciously. But after Solomon explained why they were there—not to ask about the small bill that Mr. Skatts still owed at the shop but to see about apprenticing Myer as a silversmith—as soon as Mr. Skatts heard that, he became more friendly.

He laughed, in fact, and said, "Why, I hadn't realized I still owed you anything, Mr. Myers. It must have slipped my mind. Such a small sum, really. A mere trifle. I would have paid you long ago if it hadn't slipped my mind."

"Of course, I understand," Myer's father said, just as though he really believed that Mr. Skatts had forgotten the debt. "But to get on with it, about my son, Myer. I want to apprentice him to a silversmith like yourself . . ."

"Ah yes," said Mr. Skatts, with a satisfied look around his shop. "You couldn't find a better craft for your son to learn. And as you can see, I have so much work now that I really *could* use a new apprentice. . . . How much were you thinking of paying?"

"Twenty pounds," Solomon Myers said without a moment's hesitation.

"*Twenty?*" Mr. Skatts said. "You must be joking, Mr. Myers. Why you can't buy an apprenticeship for less than forty. . . ."

"What's your lowest price?" said Solomon.

"Thirty-five," said Mr. Skatts. "Absolutely

my lowest. . . ." But his eyes gave Mr. Skatts away. They were shining brightly at the thought of getting money so unexpectedly. And the rest of his shop, in which there was hardly any work going on, gave him away too. Obviously people didn't come to him as often as they came to the more highly respected silversmiths in the city.

"Twenty-two pounds," Solomon Myers said. "I can't go any higher."

Wilhelm Skatts began to sweat. "Thirty-two," he said.

"Twenty-five," Solomon Myers said grimly.

"Thirty, then. Training an apprentice takes so much time . . . thirty pounds, and a very generous offer too."

"Twenty-seven," Solomon said.

"I *couldn't,*" Mr. Skatts almost squealed.

"Twenty-seven," said Solomon. "And, Mr. Skatts, *I'll cancel your debt at my shop in the bargain. . . .*"

Wilhelm Skatts began to smile. He wiped the sweat from his forehead and pretended to be considering the offer.

"Twenty-seven, and the debt canceled," he said at last. "All right, Mr. Myers. Consider it settled. Ordinarily I would never agree to such

an arrangment, but there are times in a man's
life when he must forget his own interests and
do something for others. Your son looks like a
fine young man. So, for his father's sake, I accept him as my apprentice. At twenty-seven
pounds, paid entirely in advance, no refund
of course in case of failure to abide by the articles of apprenticeship. Twenty-seven pounds,
and . . . my little debt canceled."

Myer and his father could hardly wait to
get away from the perspiring Mr. Skatts so
they could go home and tell the news to Myer's
mother. As soon as they could they left the
smith's shop and rushed back to Stone Street.
Once they were in the house they began to
shout and dance around the parlor like a pair
of Indians until they were finally out of breath
and had to sit down.

Then Solomon told what had happened to
Judith and to the children, how he had had to
bargain with the silversmith, and how Mr.
Skatts had rolled his eyes and pretended not
to remember the money he owned them, and
how he acted as though he was the most important and successful silversmith in the colony. The children all laughed at the way their
father imitated the hypocritical Wilhelm

Skatts, but Judith Myers laughed less than the others. "Of course I'm glad that Myer will work for him," she said. "There was nothing else we could do. All the same, I don't like to think of one of my children spending so much time with a man like that."

"But Myer won't be spending so much time with him," Solomon said. "Not if I understand anything about Mr. Skatts. Myer will be spending his time at work—while his master gets a full return out of his apprentice. I don't like the man any more than you do, but I don't think Myer will see him much, except to do his work."

Solomon Myers was right about the way that Myer had to work hard for the silversmith. But Myer didn't mind. He enjoyed it in fact, although he was often at the silversmith's from dawn till dusk, when it grew too dark to work any longer. Yet each morning, when he arrived again at Mr. Skatts's shop, it was with a fresh feeling of pleasure for the work that lay ahead. There was so much to learn before he could begin to call himself a silversmith. So much to learn before he could begin to make things himself, according to his own ideas.

During the first two years that Myer was apprenticed to Mr. Skatts he learned the elementary work of his craft. He learned how to weigh and measure the content of pure silver in an object that was to be melted down and made into something new. And once the amount was measured he learned how to melt it down properly, and how to begin to hammer the soft, heated metal into the desired shape.

But long before the object was completed the metal always began to grow stiff. It became harder and harder to work the silver. Not only that, but as the silver cooled the marks of the hammer became plain and the surface of the object rough and ugly.

Then Myer would have to reheat the unfinished object again, holding it with a pair of tongs over the fire. When the silver was hot enough the hammer marks would gradually disappear, and the metal would be soft enough to work further.

Great care had to be taken in this reheating, though. This process, called annealing, took a great deal of experience and judgment, because if it wasn't done exactly right the metal would stiffen and break into pieces under the silversmith's hammer, and all his previous work would be lost.

Myer learned not only how to anneal silver but also how to engrave letters and other insignia on the softened metal. He learned how to engrave scrollwork and other designs, and how to solder the handles on such things as teapots and tankards without leaving scars or other traces to show where the pieces had been joined.

There were, as Myer found out, more and more things to learn; for once you understood the simple things, then there was always something a little more difficult and complicated to learn next.

The first two years passed so swiftly that Myer hardly noticed they had gone by. He hardly noticed anything that was going on around him—that his brother, Asher, had suddenly shot up as tall as himself and was now apprenticed to a brazier. That his youngest sister, Rachel, was out of the cradle and could walk and run by herself. That his father hadn't been looking well and should have taken better care of himself as the doctor said.

But his father didn't take care of himself. The cough that he always had became worse quite suddenly. It was January then. Between New York and New Jersey the Hudson River was a solid sheet of ice. A cold wind and great gusts of rain swept out of the west down the bare, wet streets of the town.

Solomon Myers went out to the docks on business one January afternoon. When he returned to the shop he complained of a headache. By the time Myer returned for supper he heard his father say that his chest hurt too, and Judith held her hand on his forehead and said that he had a fever.

The doctor came and ordered Solomon to bed, where for two days and nights he rolled and tossed, the fever rising higher and higher. Judith sat by him without rest, and the children took turns bringing him soup and cold cloths to soothe his fever. The second night the doctor said their father had a lung congestion. There was very little they could do except to see that he was kept as comfortable as possible.

His condition grew worse that night. Judith sat beside him and Myer saw that the younger children were all in bed and asleep. Then the doctor came again.

It was very late when he arrived. Outside it

was raining hard. The doctor went into the bedroom and came out shaking his head.

He told Myer that it was almost over now. And Myer must be brave, he said. He must help his mother. In a few more hours she would need his help very badly.

Myer sat by the empty fireplace in the parlor wrapped up in his overcoat. His mother was upstairs in the bedroom. The house was dark, and outside the wind and the rain beat down against the windows. He tried to stay awake in case his mother called him for anything, but he was sleepy. . . .

Suddenly he was wide awake, his mother standing over him. Her hand was on his shoulder and her eyes were red, as though she had been crying. "Your father is at peace now," she said to Myer. "We will get along, somehow. You and Asher can help me. I know my sons will take their father's place."

And strangely enough it was Myer who began to cry then and his mother who tried to console him, in the room that was suddenly empty, though filled with sorrow.

The next day Judith and her children went to the Jewish burial ground to pay final honor

to her husband. They went to the same plot
of land that you may still see near Chatham
Square, on New York's Lower East Side.

The afternoon was cold and clear. The
reader of the synagogue led the service. He
read from the beautiful twenty-third psalm,
the one that says:

The Lord is my shepherd; I shall not want.
He maketh me to lie down in green pastures;
He leadeth me beside the still waters.
He restoreth my soul;
He leadeth me in the paths of righteousness
  for his name's sake.
Yea, though I walk through the valley of the
  shadow of death,
I will fear no evil,
For thou art with me;
Thy rod and thy staff, they comfort me.
Thou preparest a table before me in the pres-
  ence of mine enemies;
Thou anointest my head with oil; my cup run-
  neth over.
Surely goodness and mercy shall follow me all
  the days of my life;
And I shall dwell in the house of the Lord for
  ever.

Myer saw that his mother was crying again, but the words of the psalm brought her comfort. She was leaning on his arm, and he could almost feel the strength return to her, the wonderful strength that she had always had and that, like so many other things, he had never really noticed before.

"Your mother is a brave woman," one of the mourners said to Myer. And Myer knew it was true, more true than he had ever realized till that moment.

And that night, when he was alone with Asher, they talked about their family, and what they would do to help their mother. It would be another few years before either of them had a shop of his own. But they swore that they would work hard and take care of their mother and the younger children, now that there was no one else to look after them.

It was a sorrowful time for Myer, but sometimes sorrow can be useful too. A few days before he had still been a boy at heart. Now he had to try to fill his father's shoes. The carefree days were over. He was a man—with a man's responsibilities.

3. The Beautiful Menorah

During the next few years, while Myer and Asher were still apprenticed, the Myers family struggled to survive. They moved to another house, in a poorer section of the city. Here Judith Myers ran the shop during the day while her five younger children were away at school. In the evenings Myer and Asher went over the accounts, made out lists of goods on hand and ordered new supplies, the way they had seen their father do when he was alive. When they were not in school the younger children helped their mother in the shop, and enough money came in so that with the assistance of others they were able to stay together.

This assistance was given to them by the Jewish congregation in New York. At that time, and for many years afterward, it was the only congregation in New York, and its name was Shearith Israel.

Myer's father, Solomon, had served the congregation for several years before his death. Now the congregation remembered his widow and children. They gave Judith Myers a pension of thirty pounds a year and allowed her to continue to draw the eight cords of wood that they had always allowed to Solomon.

But even if Solomon Myers hadn't performed various chores in the synagogue, the Jewish community would have come to the assistance of his family. It was a point of honor among New York's Jews that they took care of their own people, that the almshouse and the public hospital had few if any Jewish inmates. Whenever one of their number, like

Judith Myers, fell on hard times, they never hesitated to lend a helping hand. This condition was maintained in New York for the greater part of the eighteenth century; only later, when the city was much larger and people lost touch, were Jews in misfortune ever found who had to call in any way on public charity.

Knowing that his mother was receiving a pension from the synagogue merely served as a spur to Myer to work harder than ever. As the months passed he learned more and more from Wilhelm Skatts, from watching him and from making various pieces according to his designs and instructions.

In fact, without fully realizing it himself, he had now learned all that the silversmith could teach him. For his natural talent was great, and he was able to learn far more quickly than the average apprentice. Once he had made something in a certain way, he never had to repeat the process in order to remember how it should be done. After that it became a part of an unconscious skill that he carried with him, and that he could call on at any time.

Wilhelm Skatts recognized that his young

apprentice was exceptionally gifted. At first this pleased him immensely. As he thought about it at night, and ran his fingers through his dark, oily hair, a grin would appear on his face.

So his apprentice was clever, exceptionally clever? Good! Nothing could be better—for Wilhelm Skatts!

Gradually he began to shift more of the work to Myer. First he let Myer do the rough work, the preliminaries. Then he let him do all the annealing. And Myer never overheated the metal once, or caused it to break or stain.

Then he began to place the more difficult work in Myer's hands, and still Myer performed it quickly and well. So well, in fact, that several of the pieces attracted attention. Mr. Skatts's customers had begun to talk to their friends about the excellent work he was doing.

At first most people didn't believe it. They had heard of Mr. Skatts before and knew that his work wasn't much to brag about. But now, as they looked at his latest things, they began to think they might have been wrong in saying he didn't know how to be a silversmith. Instead of automatically going to Mr. Kierstede or Mr. Wynkoop or Mr. Van Dyck, they began to order certain pieces from Mr. Skatts.

And when they came to the shop to pick up their orders, or when Myer and Mr. Skatts carried the orders to their homes, they saw that the workmanship was really of the very highest sort—and in turn they told their friends about the silversmith who worked in the house on Dock Street, not far from the wharves.

So much new work began to come into the shop now that Mr. Skatts couldn't have handled it all himself even if he had wanted to. But since he was neither a fast worker nor a good one, this sudden flood of business left him in a great dilemma. He wanted the money for doing the work—but how was he to get it all done?

Wilhelm Skatts worried about it day and night for several weeks. He knew what he had to do: he had to allow Myer even more freedom, to give him more and more important work to do in the shop.

But at the same time he hated to give him a free hand, because each day that went by he became more jealous of Myer. The young man's skill far outshone his own. Myer, hardly twenty years old, already could do things with shape and design, with lettering and scroll-work, that he, Wilhelm Skatts, couldn't do at twice his age.

Jealousy was only part of the reason that Mr. Skatts began to hate Myer, though. Not only was the boy a better craftsman, but he was largely responsible for the new business that was arriving at the shop and for the smith's new reputation as the maker of fine things. Mr. Skatts began to live in dread of the day when the truth would leak out and someone discover that it was Myer Myers and not himself who was really the author of so many lovely pieces of silver.

So Wilhelm Skatts worked out a careful plan to take care of his problems. The plan was for the present, and also for the future.

For the present he would let Myer do as much of the work as one man could possibly do. That would improve the master's reputation still further. At the same time he would make absolutely sure—by frightening Myer—that nobody should learn the secret of what was really going on in the shop.

For the future—well, here Mr. Skatts's jealousy gained control of his good sense. His plan was as evil as it was simple. He would let Myer work out almost all of his apprenticeship, and then he would accuse Myer of being a thief. Of course there wouldn't be any truth in it—but who would believe Myer, a mere apprentice, when he denied the accusation of Wilhelm Skatts, the eminent silversmith?

After that, if Myer said that Mr. Skatts didn't do his own work, people would laugh at him. Myer, discharged from the shop, would be in public disgrace. With no certificate of service, the boy couldn't go into business for himself either, and he, Wilhelm Skatts would remain the most famous silversmith in New York.

There was one mistake in the plan that Mr. Skatts didn't bother to think much about. How, after Myer left the shop, was all the work to get done?

Well, as far as that went, Wilhelm Skatts told himself, he could do it himself, and if it wasn't *always* as good as what Myer did, who would notice the difference anyway? And if they happened to notice . . . well, he would cross that bridge when he came to it.

The important thing was to get all the work possible out of Myer now, to see that nobody learned the truth about the shop and to make sure that Myer, at the last moment, was discharged in disgrace.

So one day he went to Myer, put on his broadest smile and said, "Myer, you've been doing excellent work for me these last few months. I'm very pleased."

"I'm glad you are," Myer said.

"And just to show you how pleased I am—and how fond I've become of you—I'm going to do something exceptional for you."

Myer smiled happily, for he had no real idea as yet how the silversmith felt toward him.

"What are you going to do?" Myer said.

"I'm going to let you have a free hand here, because I think you'll learn faster that way. You can make your own designs and carry out the work from first to last. Now, what do you say to that?"

"Why, I think it's wonderful," Myer said, his gray eyes bright with the sudden pleasure he felt at the news. To be on his own after only a part of his apprenticeship was served! This was more than he'd dared hope for. He could hardly wait to get home to tell his mother and Asher and the younger children. . . .

"Of course," the smith said quickly, "whatever you do will still be my work *officially*. It will bear my mark—you understand that?"

Myer nodded. He was still filled with happiness—and then he noticed that Wilhelm Skatts was looking at him sharply, and there was an ugly expression that began to grow on his face.

"I don't want you to get the wrong idea," he said to Myer. "I'm doing this as a favor to you, because I like you, and always liked your father. But if you ever tell anyone the work is your own—so that people think you're the clever one here—why you'll be very sorry, I can promise you that."

"I understand," Myer said quickly.

"So you aren't to breathe a word about it," Wilhelm Skatts told Myer, laying a large hand on his shoulder and beginning to squeeze Myer fiercely. "Not a word. Not so much as a whisper, to your mother, or your friends, or to anyone else. You understand?" And he gave Myer another squeeze, harder than the first.

"I won't tell *anyone*," Myer said.

"Because if you do—do you know what will happen to you?"

Myer shook his head.

"I'll throw you out of my shop," Wilhelm Skatts said. "I'll tell people you stole from me, that you're a thief, and then you won't be able to work as an apprentice anywhere else. You're too poor to buy another apprenticeship, so all your family's money will be wasted. Do you understand—all wasted, if you ever tell a single living soul that any of the work isn't mine?"

"I understand," Myer said again.

The smith grinned down at him and his hand relaxed its grip. "There, now we both know where we are. I'm doing you a favor by letting you learn things for yourself. And you're going to keep still about it, the way we said. And we'll both get along better than ever. As long as you don't forget your part of the bargain."

Myer had never seen such hatred on a man's face before. He realized in that second or two what Mr. Skatts was really like, that the silversmith was insanely jealous of his talent and hated him because of it. And Myer understood that it wasn't friendship that was moving Mr. Skatts to give him a free hand with the work of the shop but his love of making money. Myer saw that because of his skill he was Mr. Skatts's meal ticket as long as he was apprenticed to him—and there wasn't anything in the world he could do about it.

Myer didn't tell anyone about this meeting with Mr. Skatts, not even his mother or Asher. As far as they were concerned he was still just an apprentice at the silversmith's shop, doing much of the work, but all of it under Mr. Skatts's direction. No one, in fact, except Myer and the silversmith, knew the truth.

Myer himself was upset and confused. On the one hand, he was delighted to have complete independence at the shop, so that he didn't mind being overworked all the time. On the other hand, he knew that Wilhelm Skatts was his enemy, and spending all day with a man who hates you is never very pleasant.

And Myer was human enough to resent the unfair way Mr. Skatts was treating him. He knew he was being "used" by the silversmith to make money for him, and to further the silversmith's reputation. Myer felt a smoldering anger at this, the anger, at least in part, of a true artist. For the work he was doing now was his own—let Mr. Skatts keep the money—but each object that he made, each new salver and teapot and fork and spoon, owed its beauty solely to Myer's skill.

Myer grew angry every time he thought of how his own work had to go unrecognized in the world. But he was afraid to say anything about it. He knew that if Mr. Skatts ever learned that Myer had told the truth about him, he would throw Myer out of his shop as a thief before he had finished his apprenticeship. Then all the money that Myer's parents had saved would be lost, and all their hopes for him would come to an end. So he curbed his anger and held his silence.

One afternoon, as Myer was hard at work, the little bell above the door of the shop rang loudly, signaling the arrival of a customer. As usual, Mr. Skatts went to the front of the shop to see who was there. Myer looked up from the fire and saw that it was Isaac Seixas, one of his father's friends, and one of the most important members of the Jewish community.

He was by far the richest man to come to Wilhelm Skatts's shop since Myer had been there. Mr. Skatts knew his importance and was sure that if Isaac Seixas left an order, and was pleased with it afterward, his good word with other rich and prominent customers could be expected.

So Mr. Skatts smiled, rubbed his hands together and rolled his eyes as he stood in the doorway. He made a low bow and said, "Ah, Mr. Seixas, what a splendid day this is for my shop. The first time that I've been honored by your presence, and I hope, by your patronage."

"I'm here to place an order, if that's what you mean," Isaac said in a dry voice.

"Splendid, Mr. Seixas. I'm proud to put the skill of my craft at the disposal of such a man as you. One with such refined taste, one who—"

"One who has the money to order something in silver," Isaac said. He looked around the shop and saw the apprentice standing by the fireplace.

"Myer, I'm glad to see you," Isaac said, leaving the front of the shop and walking over to shake hands with him. "I've been meaning to call at your mother's house to see how she was getting on. I knew your father quite well. I admired him."

Isaac Seixas looked Myer up and down. He saw that Myer was tall and spare and rather handsome with his dark hair and steady gray eyes. Then he turned back to Mr. Skatts, who was wiping his brow and stirring anxiously around the shop as he waited to receive the order.

"Mr. Skatts," Isaac said, "I've come here because I've been hearing some interesting things about you and your shop."

Wilhelm Skatts looked scared for a second, but he hid his fear quickly. "Interesting things about me?" he said.

"That's right. I've heard that you've been doing some very fine work for your customers. Really fine. So I've decided to give you a chance to have my trade. It isn't large, but from time to time I like to have something done in silver. My buckles and buttons of course, and other things."

"I'm honored, honored," Wilhelm Skatts said.

"So I've come to place my first order with you. Perform it to my satisfaction, and you'll have my business from now on."

"You'll be satisfied, depend on it," Wilhelm Skatts practically shouted in a fit of delight and nervousness. "Now, what is your first order to be, Mr. Seixas? A cream jug, some silver plate, or perhaps something larger? A teapot, a bowl . . . ?"

"No," Isaac Seixas said. "I want you to make me a religious object. In time for Hanukkah. A Menorah, that's the name we Jews give to our candleholders. I don't know if you've seen any . . ."

"Oh I have, I have," Wilhelm Skatts said. "I'm very familiar with Menorahs. Now, sir, do you have any particular design, any special style in mind?"

Isaac Seixas shook his head. "You're the craftsman. I want something simple and graceful. I leave the details up to you."

"Of course, that's what I'm here for," Mr. Skatts said. "You're right to leave the details up to me. You won't regret it. I have a design in mind already. . . . I can almost see it now, before my eyes . . . simple, but very graceful. . . . And now, Mr. Seixas, about the cost. If you would just step inside my parlor, I'm sure we can make the arrangements in no time at all."

Isaac followed Wilhelm Skatts inside the parlor, where they talked for several minutes before returning to the shop again. On his way out Isaac nodded to Myer and said, "I've been hearing nothing but good things about you, Myer. I hope they're true. We'll probably meet again soon." And then his spare figure disappeared into the street.

Wilhelm Skatts began to pace up and down the shop as soon as Isaac Seixas was gone. "A Menorah, a Menorah," he said. "Well, well, well, we shall have to see. . . . I *could* do it myself, but I have so many other things on my mind. . . .

"Myer! Come here. . . . I want to discuss this with you. . . ."

Myer knew that Mr. Skatts was afraid to do the Menorah himself. There was very little time left, to finish it before Hanukkah. Even more important was the fact that nothing so large or complicated had been ordered in the shop for years. Mr. Skatts was certainly afraid to do it. So Myer wasn't surprised when the silversmith said he was going to do Myer a "favor" and let him design and complete the Menorah on his own.

"For one thing, it will be good training for you," he said to Myer. "And for another, you're a Jew, so you should have more feeling for your own religious objects than a Christian would have. So . . . you go ahead and start it, and ask me if you have any questions."

Myer worked most of the next two days and nights planning the Menorah. It was the greatest challenge that he had ever had at the shop, and at first he was afraid that his design and workmanship would not please Isaac Seixas. But once he had a picture of the Menorah in mind he forgot his fears. He began to work at a furious pace, shaping the base of the Menorah first, then the arms and finally the cups to hold the sacred candles. He made the base round and broad, and the arms thin and curved, and when the Menorah was finished except for the final buffing and polishing, his heart was proud.

It was a beautiful design, as beautiful as he had dreamed it would be from the beginning. Now, if only he didn't mar the surface, the job would be complete.

Hanukkah began the next evening but one. Myer worked like a demon. He buffed and polished with extreme care. His fingers worked deftly, with all the skill they had acquired during his years in the shop. And while he worked, he hardly noticed what was going on around him. He didn't notice Wilhelm Skatts pacing up and down, or peering anxiously over his shoulder at the Menorah.

Finally, just before sunset on the day before Hanukkah, the work was done. Myer sat up straight and set the Menorah on the table. He seemed to be waking up, as if from a deep sleep, and he was able to look at his work and judge it for the first time.

The sheen on the metal was extraordinary. It completed the design of the Menorah itself, and set off and enhanced its beauty.

Wilhelm Skatts looked at the Menorah and said, "So you've finished at last, Myer. And none too soon. We'll take it over to Mr. Seixas now. You'll carry it. And be sure you don't drop it. Anything for Mr. Seixas must be letter perfect."

Myer put on his hat and coat and followed Mr. Skatts into the street. He suddenly felt tired and empty after the strain of work. So tired that when he heard Mr. Skatts say, "And remember, Myer, this is my design and my workmanship—not a word about your working on it," he was too exhausted to feel his usual anger at the cunning and deceit of the silversmith.

Inside Mr. Seixas' parlor they were greeted by Isaac himself. Mr. Skatts seized his hand and said enthusiastically, "I know you're going to like what I've brought you, Mr. Seixas. Here, Myer, don't be so clumsy. Take more care with the wrappings. Pull them off slowly. You know how I told you this was an important piece I was making for Mr. Seixas."

When the wrappings were unwound and the Menorah stood on Isaac's polished table, Myer looked at it again and was struck a second time by the beauty of the work he had done. He had never felt this way before, but the Menorah, for some reason, seemed special, and he knew that if he had been able to he would have liked to keep this one thing that he had made, for himself.

Then he looked at Isaac to see what he thought of the Menorah. Isaac Seixas was a quiet person, so it was hard to guess what he was thinking. He looked at the Menorah, picked it up by the base, then set it down again on the table. The gleaming wood seemed to add even greater brilliance to the silver object resting on it. Then Isaac walked around the table and examined the Menorah from all

sides, and finally he said, "It's very handsome.
The handsomest Menorah I've ever seen. I'm
pleased. Completely. I wonder, Mr. Skatts, if
you will do me the pleasure of stopping for a
glass of wine?"

It wasn't so much an invitation as an order,
and Wilhelm Skatts was only too eager to obey.
A frown appeared on his face for just a second, though, when he heard Isaac add, "And
let's have your young apprentice join us too."

After they were served the wine they sat
down in the parlor. Myer took a sip and felt
the wine go right to his head. He was still dizzy
from lack of sleep anyway, and at first he
wasn't even aware that Isaac was looking at
Mr. Skatts and questioning him.

"Quite a remarkable piece of work you've
done for me," Isaac was saying. "Really quite
extraordinary."

"I always aim at the highest standards of
workmanship," Wilhelm Skatts said.

"I can see that," Isaac said. "Though according to what people say, you didn't *always*
aim at such high standards, Mr. Skatts."

The silversmith stirred uneasily. "I don't
know what you mean, Mr. Seixas. . . ."

"I mean that until the last year or two, your reputation wasn't as good as some of the other silversmiths in the city."

"Certain people have always been against me. You know how tongues can wag . . . ruin a man's good name. . . ."

"Now tell me," Isaac said, looking back at the Menorah, "how much did Myer have to do with this? Did you let him work on it?"

"On *your* Menorah?" Wilhelm Skatts protested. "Never! Not once! Not for a second! Do you seriously think, Mr. Seixas, that I would trust a raw apprentice with something so important?"

Isaac was walking, glass in hand, around the table again. The truth was, he suspected that the Menorah was probably Myer's work and not the silversmith's. A rumor had been making the rounds of the city lately. A rumor that said what a strange coincidence it was that Mr. Skatts's workmanship had started to improve only after a boy named Myer Myers had been apprenticed to him. How, people asked, could a man who for twenty years had been making shoddy goods suddenly turn into a truly fine artist? Wasn't it just possible that the apprentice was doing the work and the master taking the credit?

Isaac Seixas had heard the rumor for quite a time. He had even discussed it with other men who had been Solomon Myers' friends. And he had learned, from a talk with Judith Myers, that for the last few months Myer had avoided discussing anything about the work he did at the shop, as if he was afraid to reveal what was actually happening there.

Isaac Seixas had grown angry at the thought that the son of his friend Solomon might be ill-used by the silversmith. So, as part of his plan to learn the truth, he had ordered the Menorah.

Myer hadn't been watching Isaac very closely as the tall man circled the table, and when he heard his own name spoken he had to shake himself and focus his attention.

"Myer," Isaac was saying, "Mr. Skatts tells me that this Menorah is entirely his own work. That you had nothing to do with it? Is that true?"

"Yes, it is, Mr. Seixas," Myer said quickly.

"You're sure?"

"Yes, I am."

Isaac Seixas was staring at him, and Myer couldn't bear to meet his glance. His eyes were dark and amazingly steady. They were the eyes of an honest man, the kind that you can't bear to meet if you have to tell a lie.

Isaac Seixas paused, and waited till Myer had to look at him again. Then he said, "Myer, you're afraid of something. Whatever it is, you have no cause to fear. I'm your friend. You can trust me. Now tell me, Myer, because I'm asking you again. Did you have anything to do with making that Menorah?"

Myer hesitated, torn between a desire to blurt out the truth and the dread of Wilhelm Skatts's anger if he revealed it. He feared for himself and for his mother and for the others in his family. He would be disgraced; Mr. Skatts had promised him that. He would be without a job and without a trade, with no hope for the future, and no way of helping his mother or his younger brothers or sisters. . . .

"Did you have anything to do with making it?" Isaac asked him again. "In fact, Myer, did you design and make it yourself, while Mr. Skatts stood by, ready to take the credit?"

"But . . . how outrageous!" Wilhelm Skatts

said. He rose to his feet threateningly, but there was something about Isaac Seixas that made him lower his arms and calm his voice. "Outrageous. Do you think a boy, an apprentice, could make such a thing? Why, Mr. Seixas . . ."

But Isaac was still staring at Myer, gripping him with his eyes. "Tell me, Myer. The truth is always better for being spoken."

Myer shook his head, but remained silent.

Then Isaac Seixas said with anger, "You're a coward, Myer. Only a coward hides the truth because he's afraid to speak."

Myer looked into Isaac Seixas' face. He knew the older man was right—he was afraid. But he was stung by the word "coward." With a sick feeling he rose slowly to his feet and said, "You told me you were my friend, Mr. Seixas. I believe you. I hope I'm doing right when I trust you. I *am* afraid—for my mother and my family. They need my help—but what would you know about that? Anyway, I don't care what happens now. I *was* telling you a lie. The Menorah is mine. All of it. From first to last. I did all the work—Mr. Skatts never even touched it."

Myer sank back in his chair and shut his eyes. He could hear Wilhelm Skatts stamp his foot and roar like a wounded bull.

"The boy's insane, a liar from beginning to end. I'll have him arrested and clapped in the fort. He's a thief, and I can prove it. He's been stealing from me, a little at a time, for months. I would have thrown him out long before this, but I felt sorry for his mother, a poor widow. But now he's gone too far. I'll tell this to the whole town, I'll tell the whole world about this lying, cheating boy—"

"You'd better not tell anything to anyone," Isaac Seixas said evenly. "You'd better pick up your hat and coat, Mr. Skatts, and leave this house as quickly as possible. And if you *do* say anything, if you try to spread your lies any further, I'll drive you from the city in a week. I'll tell people what you really are. I have a certain reputation for honesty, Mr. Skatts. I don't think you'd better challenge my word in public."

Myer saw the silversmith disappear, and then he looked at Isaac Seixas. Isaac was smiling for the first time. "Now, Myer," he said, "the truth is out, and I'm sure you feel better because of it."

Myer nodded. "Yes—except for Mr. Skatts."

"He won't be able to do anything to you," Isaac said.

"It's losing my apprenticeship," Myer told him. "I can't go into business for myself yet. . . . I don't know what I'll do . . . and my mother was counting on my help."

"I told you I was your friend," Isaac said. "Trust me. In a few days I think your troubles will be over."

"I'm sure they will," Myer said, but he said it mostly out of politeness.

Actually, he didn't see how things could be much worse. His apprenticeship was lost, and his parents' money lost along with it. He couldn't bear to think of the future, which had looked so bright up until a few minutes before.

Myer left Isaac Seixas' house and returned home. He told his mother all that had happened, and Judith Myers said, "Well, one thing is true, Myer. Isaac Seixas is an honest man. Let's hope he's true to his word and does something to help you now."

"Let's hope so," Myer said. But in his heart there wasn't much room for anything but the darkest feelings. As far as Myer could see, he

had reached a dead end. At twenty his life was
in ruins. At least that was the way things
looked to him as he said good night and slowly
went upstairs.

4. A Young Man in the City

The next week was the most agonizing that Myer had ever known. Each morning he woke up and thought at once of Isaac Seixas. Isaac had promised help—then why was there no word from him? Isaac had said that he was Myer's friend—well, what was he doing to prove it?

Myer had always been quick-tempered, and now his anger flashed out against Isaac. He walked around the house repeating Isaac's name and demanding to know why he had urged Myer to tell the truth and then had backed out on his promise to come to his aid.

Judith Myers and Asher tried to calm him down. Asher had always been easygoing, so it was natural for him to say, "Be a little patient, Myer. You're always in such a rush. And you always look on the dark side of things. It's only been a few days. You'll hear from Mr. Seixas before much longer."

That's just like Asher, Myer thought. Be patient—while the world's falling down around your head.

Each day that week Myer thought of Isaac Seixas and his promise to help. But as the days dragged by and no word came, he fell into despair.

He had no place to work now. Mr. Skatts's shop was closed to him. So he sat in his mother's store and took care of her customers. And it seemed to Myer that the people who came into the store avoided looking at him, as if there were something the matter with him. He began to feel certain that Mr. Skatts had spread his lies all over town, and that people thought he was really a thief.

Once or twice Myer left the shop to walk around the streets of the city. But he felt embarrassed, thinking that Wilhelm Skatts had told his lies everywhere. Each time he heard someone laugh he was sure they were laughing at him. And before he had been out ten minutes, he turned and rushed home again and sat behind the counter the rest of the day, dreading the sound of approaching footsteps and the appearance of another customer.

Seven days passed like this, and on the afternoon of the eighth, the last day of Hanukkah, Judith Myers came into the shop and said to Myer, "We must all get dressed. We're going out for supper."

"Where are we going?" Myer said with surprise.

"To Isaac Seixas' house. I met him outside the synagogue and he invited all of us to celebrate the holiday with him tonight. So you see, maybe Asher and I were right. Maybe he hasn't forgotten his promise after all."

With new hope, Myer put on his best clothes, and then went out with his mother and Asher and the five younger children to

Mr. Seixas' house. Once inside, they all sat down for supper. Isaac Seixas read a prayer as he stood over by the sideboard near the window. On the sideboard stood the Menorah that Myer had made for him. It was placed near the window, so that in keeping with tradition, the light from its candles could be seen from outside the house.

Isaac lit the candles one by one, until all eight had been lit. Then he returned to the table and everyone began to eat—but still he said nothing about the troubles that were making Myer so miserable.

Isaac talked with Judith Myers and with Myer and Asher, but not once did he mention Wilhelm Skatts. The minutes dragged by and Myer felt sure that Isaac had forgotten him.

Only when the meal was over did a new expression appear on Isaac's face. Then he said to the youngest children, to Sarah and Rebecca and Rachel, "Do you see that Menorah over against the wall?"

The girls nodded.

"Do you know who made it?"

"Our brother, Myer," they said.

"Yes, he made it for me, so that I could use it this year to celebrate Hanukkah. That's why

I asked you here—to have supper with me and to hear the story of your brother's Menorah."

Isaac cleared his throat and looked around at the children. "You all know why we Jews celebrate Hanukkah each year," he said. "We do it to commemorate the bravery of the famous Maccabees, who lived centuries and centuries ago, in Palestine. They were very brave men. They refused, as some of their fellow Jews were doing, to give up their customs and beliefs for the sake of pleasing the rulers of the country. And when the temple in Jerusalem was desecrated, they rose up and declared war on their oppressors. They fought them in the hills, first with little more than their bare hands and then with weapons that they captured from the enemy. They fought for many years, and finally, because they were so few and their enemies so many, they were defeated.

"But," Isaac continued, "the important thing was that by standing up and fighting they preserved their beliefs, so that really they weren't defeated at all. Their name has come down to us, and we do them honor each year, and try to keep our own beliefs as pure and uncorrupted as theirs.

"Now," Isaac said, "there are many kinds of bravery in the world. There's the bravery of the Maccabees, where a man must take up arms to fight his enemies. But there is another kind of bravery too, the kind that most of us are called on to show at some time in our lives. Do you know what this second kind of bravery is?"

Everyone was silent, and the little girls shook their heads.

"It's the bravery that forces a man to speak the truth, even when he knows the truth can hurt him. When he knows that his enemies will speak lies against him and insult him and try to destroy him. When he knows that his own well-being and that of this family may be put in danger if he speaks the truth.

"Now that's what your brother did," Isaac Seixas said, "when he told me that he had made the Menorah that you see over there. Your brother, Myer, knew that his enemy was listening to every word he said. He knew that his enemy had threatened to punish him terribly if he told the truth. But Myer told it anyway—in spite of the fact that he was frightened and wanted to protect himself and his family.

"So I shall keep the Menorah that your

brother made for me," Isaac said, "and whenever I look at it, or whenever I use it, I will remember his kind of bravery too, and I will be as proud of Myer as we Jews have always been of the Maccabees."

Isaac turned to Myer now. "I said I was your friend. I told you I would help you. Now listen to what I've done, and see if you're satisfied."

All eyes were fixed on Isaac Seixas. "I've been to see Benjamin Wynkoop," he said to Myer. "He knows who you are, and what happened between you and Wilhelm Skatts. Mr. Wynkoop says he will be glad to accept you as his apprentice. But you won't have to start over and serve for seven years more. You'll only have to be with him the same length of time that you would have been with Wilhelm Skatts.

"So, in another three years, you will be finished with your apprenticeship and can set up a shop of your own. And when that time comes, you and your mother and I will discuss the matter and decide where your shop should be, and how you're to be launched into business for yourself."

Myer remembered the way he had been secretly cursing Isaac Seixas all week, and he felt his cheeks begin to burn with shame. He started to thank Isaac now, but Isaac waved his hand for silence.

"You don't owe me anything, Myer," he said. "If you want to thank anyone, thank your mother. I met her outside the synagogue to-day, and she told me she had been praying for you. Maybe through me some of her prayers are being answered now. At any rate, your mother said something to me today that we should all remember. 'God,' your mother said, 'looks after us, if we remember God. But when we forget Him, then it always seems as if He has forgotten us.'

"So, Myer, if things have turned out happily for you, it isn't just because of me, or your mother, or yourself. God does look after his children, only sometimes, at first, it's hard to understand the mysterious ways in which he works. Something will happen that hurts us very much; only later do we understand that it's done us some good too. Like your troubles with Wilhelm Skatts. Now that they're over, who can say if it wasn't all for the best?"

So at last everything was arranged, and Myer found that all his old fears were behind him. And when he was alone in his room later that night, he thought of Isaac Seixas and the Menorah, and of the many things that Isaac had said at the table. And in his heart he thanked God for his good fortune, for the chance to work out his apprenticeship with Mr. Wynkoop, and most of all, for the kindness of Isaac to him and his family.

It was almost as if, it seemed to Myer, that God Himself had taken a hand in the affair and, through Isaac, had helped him overcome all the obstacles in his path. He had never thought of God in that way before. He had always thought that God belonged in the Bible and in the synagogue, but not really in a person's everyday life. He remembered his mother's words: "God looks after us—if we remember God."

Myer knew that was why he had despaired so easily. He had forgotten God's strength and God's love. It pained him to think of the sort of person he had become. And that night he made a vow to change himself if he could, and to try to remember God in good times as well as in bad, the way that people like his mother seemed to do.

The next three years were the happiest that Myer had known since childhood. He was apprenticed to Benjamin Wynkoop, who never tried to take advantage of him. Mr. Wynkoop was an able craftsman and made a good living as a smith. He liked Myer and was pleased to discover how great his skills were. He taught Myer all that he could, and saw to it that he had important pieces to work on, so that when the time came for Myer to go into business for himself, he would have enough experience to handle even the most difficult commissions.

Finally, when the three years were up, Mr. Wynkoop signed Myer's release from apprenticeship, and welcomed him as an equal into the city's band of silversmiths. And shortly afterward, with the help of Isaac Seixas, who loaned him the necessary funds, Myer took a house of his own and set up his shop on lower Wall Street.

Myer was on top of the world that day in early May when he unlocked the door of his own shop for the first time and heard the tinkle of the bell over the door . . . the same sound he had heard ten years before, when he had run an errand for one of his father's customers and, coming into Mr. Van Dyck's shop, had seen the gleam of polished silver on every side. Now, ten years later, he was a silversmith himself. With his own shop, his own fireplace, his own tools.

Myer was bending over, trying to get the fire started, when the bell by the door rang again. He looked up and saw his mother walk in followed by their friend, Isaac Seixas.

They came over to the fireplace, and Judith Myers sat down in one of the new chairs while Isaac looked at Myer and said, "Any customers yet?"

"Not yet," Myer said.

"Good," said Isaac. "Then maybe I'll be your first."

He pretended to frown, and acted as if he were a stranger who didn't know anything about Myer's skill. "I want half a dozen spoons," he said. "They have to be the best." Isaac's frown grew even darker. "Delicate, but sturdy. Do you think you can make the spoons for me?"

"I'm sure that I can," Myer said, acting as though he were talking to a stranger too.

"Well . . . ordinarily I wouldn't come to anyone as young as you," Isaac said. "But I heard about you from a man whose opinion I trust. Fellow named Isaac Seixas. He told me the other day that you were quite skillful already. So we'll see. Make me the spoons, and I'll know if Isaac Seixas was right or not."

Then Isaac laughed and wrote down his order and signed his name underneath, the way a customer always did when he placed an order at a silversmith's. And Myer returned to the fireplace and lit the fire, and soon afterward began to work on the first commission he had received in his own shop. Six silver spoons that would bear his mark, MM, for the first time.

After that Isaac Seixas did Myer many good turns, especially at the beginning of his career when Myer needed help the most. Isaac not only ordered all his silver there, but told his friends about Myer's skill and urged them to bring their trade to his shop.

Business came in, slowly but steadily. Myer wasn't an overnight success, because he was still very young, and people are usually slow to recognize a new artist. With men like Benjamin Wynkoop and Pieter Van Dyck still working in New York, men who had been known there for years, people were reluctant to take their orders to an unknown silversmith just starting out in the trade.

Still, his commissions grew in number and importance, and Myer began to make a modest living. He did well enough so that he was able to help his mother the way he had always planned to, and before very long, with Myer himself in complete agreement, the Jewish congregation, Shearith Israel, was able to reduce Judith's pension to twenty pounds a year. And before too many years had passed, Myer and his brother, Asher, were able to support their mother and younger sisters completely, and the pension at last was discontinued.

As soon as Myer saw that he was going to get along as a silversmith, his thoughts naturally turned to getting married and starting a family. Almost at once his eye fell on a girl named Rachel Levy. She was one of the prettiest girls in the city, and Myer fell head-over-heels in love with her.

He courted her for a year, brought her presents and took her out walking on summer afternoons. Rachel had many other suitors, but Myer told himself that his chances were very good, because she gave every sign of being fond of him.

Finally he could bear to wait no longer. He told her how much he loved her, and asked for her hand. He saw Rachel turn away from him and hesitate. When she finally spoke, she said she was still too young to think of marriage, and her parents thought so too. They wanted her to wait at least a year before making up her mind. Myer hid his disappointment and resolved to be patient.

One day, less than a month later, Asher came into Myer's shop and sat down near the fire. At first he pretended that he was just there to pass the time of day. Then he shifted in his chair and said, trying to keep his voice matter-of-fact, that he had heard a story about Rachel Levy. In fact, he had heard it from several people . . . Rachel was getting married . . . it was all over town.

At first Myer couldn't believe it. He was sure Asher was telling him the truth, yet the truth seemed impossible.

"But Rachel said she didn't want to get married yet," Myer told his brother. "She said she was too young. She told me so herself."

"When you asked her to marry you?"

Myer nodded. "I thought she cared for me, Asher . . . she always said she did . . . she pretended to . . . I can't understand why she should do this now."

"It's very simple," Asher said. He was trying to be kind to his brother, but at the same time he wanted Myer to see the truth. "Everyone says the same thing about Rachel. And they always *have* said it."

"What do they say?" Myer asked.

"They say that Rachel Levy has a cold heart. She's only getting married now because she can make a good match. The man is very rich —that's why someone like you, Myer, never really had a chance with her. I've heard at least a dozen people say the same thing. She's a girl who wants to get married for money, because nothing else matters to her."

Myer didn't say another word. He turned back to his work table and went on hammering the silver he was shaping, just as though the news meant nothing to him.

But inside he was filled with bitterness and humiliation. He thought of how ridiculous he must have looked, all during the months he had been courting Rachel. He imagined how she must have laughed at him secretly, knowing that she would never have anything to do with someone who was only starting out in life, with no fortune at his command.

And how heartless she had been, telling him that she was too young to marry—and not that he was simply too poor for her taste.

It's always a question of money, Myer thought. Lack of it made my father unhappy all the last years of his life. Lack of it forced him to apprentice me to Wilhelm Skatts, and all my own misery came as the result. Money is the one element in life that a man needs for happiness. Nothing else matters. The rest is just cant and hypocrisy.

Myer looked up from his work, and when he did, his jaw was set firmly. Asher saw the strange look on his face. He said to Myer, "Is anything the matter? Are you all right?"

Myer smiled grimly and nodded his head. "Of course I am," he said. "Believe me, Asher, for the first time in my life I'm *really* all right. Because from now on, I'm going to have money. I'm going to be rich. And then . . . well, life will be different from what it's been before. . . ."

Myer's work kept him busier than ever after that. He slaved from morning till night at the shop, and never quit till the light from the windows failed and he had to go and light the candles to brighten the room. Sometimes he went without lunch and sometimes he didn't eat supper till ten o'clock, in order not to waste any of the late summer twilight.

And then there were all sorts of other activities to keep him occupied and help him forget his troubles. He was a full member of the Congregation Shearith Israel, and had responsibilities there. And he also had to take care of his mother. In time he moved her from their old house to a nicer one in a better part of the city.

Public activities took up much of his time. The city was changing, growing bigger. Wharves were built farther up the East River and farther up the Hudson. A lawless element came in on the ships—Myer realized now what most of the sailors were really like, a tough, rum-drinking crew that often caused trouble.

Gangs of sailors roamed the streets at night, brawling and fighting. They broke the street lamps put up by private citizens and they wrenched the doorknobs off the fronts of the houses. There was no police force to stop them, only the Night Watch, made up of citizens like Myer himself.

Myer always served on the Watch, whenever his turn came round. All householders had to serve, or find a substitute, but Myer and most of his fellow Jews refused to find substitutes. They were proud that after a long fight Jews were considered equal citizens in public affairs and were now granted the right to maintain the public safety. So Myer went out when his turn came and sometimes traded blows with the sailors, and was thankful that he was tall and quick on his feet and had strong hands and arms to protect himself.

At that time there was a great fear of fires in the city. Many of the houses were still made of wood, and with narrow streets affording little space between them, there was a threat to the entire city in almost every fire that started. This kept the Watch on its rounds every night of the year, ready at any time to sound the alarm.

In addition to the fear of fire, there was also the threat of attack by neighboring Indian tribes. In 1745 this threat seemed so dangerous that a palisade of timber was built on the northern side of New York City, from the Hudson to the East River. The palisade was made of cedar logs fourteen feet long, with holes in the logs to permit muskets to be passed through and fired. At intervals in the palisade there were blockhouses, the three largest rising ten feet above the palisade. On top of these towers a guard was kept to alert the citizens and the troops in the fort in case of attack.

Although the city was fortunate and no attack on the palisade ever came, it was one more sign of the dangers of the times. The palisade reminded everyone who lived in New York that England and France were locked in a struggle for the control of North America, and that the Indians were being used, some on one side, some on the other, as instruments in the struggle. With the palisade stretching from one side of Manhattan Island to the other, the thought of war and bloodshed could never be far away.

Living in such exciting times, Myer began to forget the full bitterness of disappointment that Rachel Levy had caused him. All around he saw men his own age, and men a good deal younger, getting married and having children. So, in time, he began to think again of marriage for himself.

It was now 1752, and Myer was twenty-nine years old. He began to appear more in public, often with an unmarried young lady on his arm. He courted this girl and that, was sure he was in love a dozen times, but always at the last moment he drew back.

He told himself that none of the girls he knew were quite right for him. It was better to wait a while longer. But it was really his unhappy memory of Rachel Levy that kept him from finding a wife.

One night he went to Asher's house for supper. Asher had finished his apprenticeship and was already making a name for himself as a brazier. He had been married a year, and he and his wife, Caty, had talked about Myer many times, and the fact that he was still a bachelor.

Like most young women who are happily married themselves. Caty wanted to see that everyone else was happily married too. It was her idea to have Myer there for supper and to invite a girl named Elkalah Cohen at the same time.

"She's very pretty," Caty had said when she and Asher first discussed it.

"But she's so young," Asher said.

"That's just what Myer thinks," Caty laughed. "We talked a little about her the other day, and he said that Elkalah is still a child. But Asher, she's seventeen—and plenty of girls get married at seventeen."

"Well, maybe you're right," Asher said. "It can't hurt to bring them together."

And Caty said, "Of course it can't. At the synagogue, or in the street when she's all bundled up, she *looks* like a child. Her mother doesn't know how to dress her anyway. But here at supper, with a party dress, and some candles on the table . . . well, you just wait and see. Maybe Myer won't think she's such a child after he spends an evening with her."

So Myer appeared for supper—and got one of the surprises of his life. At first he could hardly believe that Elkalah Cohen, this lively little creature sitting beside him, could be the same shy little girl he had passed on the street so often and tipped his hat to and smiled down on from his great height, the way a successful businessman smiles down on a child. Because she really wasn't a child any longer. She was

a sweet, unspoiled young lady, on the thresh-
old of womanhood.

Myer found himself staring at her so in-
tently that he made her blush. And this made
him awkward in turn. He looked away and
spent the rest of the evening talking to Caty
to hide his own embarrassment.

Afterward, when they were alone, Elkalah
told Caty that she was sure Myer didn't care
for her because he hadn't looked at her or
talked with her for hours.

But Caty reassured her. "Asher was like that
too, the first time we spent an evening together," Caty said. "I guess it's something that
runs in the Myers family. The more one of
them likes a woman, the less he has to do with
her at first. But wait and see. I think you made
a good impression on him all the same."

As for Myer, he knew that he had finally
found the woman he had been waiting for,
and if he had believed that she would accept
him, he would have rushed to her father's
house and asked for her hand. But he didn't
think she cared especially for him, so he kept
his feeling to himself.

He thought that nobody suspected what
those feelings were, but Caty and even Asher

knew the truth from the first night. They made sure that Myer and Elkalah met again, and did everything to bring the match about. Myer himself began to stop in at the Cohens' whenever he had a free moment. Finally one night he stopped there and found Elkalah alone. Her eyes seemed to shine brightly as soon as she saw him. Her friendliness gave him courage. As they sat together on the sofa he said, "I'm much older than you are, Elkalah. . . . I'm almost thirty. . . ."

He never knew how he got the rest of the words out, nor exactly what he said, but by the time her father and mother came in a few minutes later, Myer and Elkalah were ready to tell them that they loved each other and wanted to be married. Their engagement was announced, and they were married before three months had passed.

On their wedding day, everyone could see that Judith Myers was almost as happy as the newlyweds themselves. "God has looked after me," she said to Asher. "My children are getting married and having children of their own. I ask nothing else but to see all of you married and raising your own families."

Then she turned and said to Myer, who was

feeling all of the confusion that a man feels on his wedding day, "This is the most important moment of your life, Myer. From now on you'll be a different person. Elkalah will be the making of you. A good woman can do that for a man—and she's a good woman."

Myer agreed with what his mother said, then and afterward. He took his bride home to their house on Wall Street, where they settled down to marriage in the little rooms over his shop. And the months flew by. The months flew by so quickly that Myer no longer tried to keep track of them.

He had never known such happiness. Elkalah seemed to grow prettier than ever. She ran the house, set his table, cooked his food and kept his clothes in order. And with all that, they began to raise a family. Their first child was born and they named it Solomon, in honor of Myer's father.

Myer worked even harder now. Though he was beginning to do well, he was more anxious than ever to be rich, because he couldn't forget the early poverty he had known and the disappointments he had suffered because of it.

He didn't tell himself this. He told himself, I love my work, that's why I work so hard. And

it was true—he did love his work. But he
wanted to be rich too. Rich enough so that he
would never be unhappy or looked down on
again.

When Myer saw what a fine home he had
now, he was more certain than ever that money
was the key to all happiness. Without it a man
was nothing. With it he was respected and
honored on all sides, and he could make his
family happy with it too.

This is what Myer believed in his heart as
the years began to slip by. If he had any doubts
about the way he was living, he never let those
doubts come out. He had decided to become
rich—and he was getting there. And once he
was rich enough, he swore that no one would
ever be able to hurt him again.

PART TWO

THE LATE YEARS

5. Elkalah and Joyce

The next ten or twelve years were important ones in the history of North America; they saw the fourth and final outbreak of war between the French and the English, and the eventual surrender of the French in 1763. With that surrender French influence ended and English rule became supreme.

But for the people of New York, like Myer and his family, the war was distant. It was fought in such places as the Ohio River Valley and eastern Canada, at Fort Pitt and along the Mississippi, at places that meant little in themselves to the merchants and traders of the rapidly growing port of New York.

The people of New York supported the English, for most of them were English colonists and stood to gain from the defeat of the French. But in the city all remained peaceful, business flourished and the war itself seemed far away.

During these years Myer began to realize many of his ambitions. He became an honored member of the community and a leader in the synagogue. Although he was still only modestly wealthy, he was far better off than a good many other people in the city.

His family was getting bigger. There were four children by now: Solomon, Samuel, Joseph and Judith. The youngest, Judith, was born in May of 1762 and was named for Myer's mother. Their only other daughter, Ritzel, had been born two years earlier and had died in infancy, the way so many children did in the eighteenth century.

The death of Ritzel was almost the only sorrow that Myer and Elkalah knew in the dozen years of their marriage. They quarreled at times, as all people must, but their serious differences were few. Myer still found his wife as lovely and charming as ever, and full of pretty ways. She put flowers on their dining table and sewed covers for the furniture, and made their home a cheerful place to be. Even after a dozen years Myer still found delight in coming upstairs at night and taking his wife in his arms, and making her blush like a schoolgirl by whispering compliments in her ear till she made him stop, protesting that they were old married people now and should act with a little more dignity.

Elkalah had only one complaint that she made to Myer. He didn't spend enough time with her at home, she said. Often she asked him to leave his workshop early and take a walk with her, or come and sit beside her in the parlor of their new house. But Myer always said no, he was too busy. Maybe he would come later, at night, when he was finished work.

Elkalah said that the nights weren't enough —she wanted to see more of her husband. And she frowned and pretended to be angry with him until he promised to give up working so hard and spend more time with his wife and children.

She teased him, and he promised, but he never seemed to remember it the next day. Instead, he spent an extra hour over a beautiful salver that he was designing, a salver that he told himself would be the finest one he had ever made. He told himself that the beauty of it fascinated him, and not the money he would receive when it was done. And Elkalah stared at his empty place at the table, and then, after the children had eaten and been put to bed, she came downstairs and kept his food warm till Myer finally appeared for supper.

Then, trying to hide the tears in her eyes, she said that he was late, later than usual. And Myer said, "Don't cry. Tomorrow I'll stop working an hour early to make up for it."

"But we spend so little time together," she said. And Myer answered carelessly, "Why, what are you talking about? We have all the time in the world together. What difference does an hour or two make now?"

Myer was to remember his words a few months later. It was one of the things that hurt him most—to remember what he had said to his wife when she pleaded with him to share more of his life with her—and he had ignored her pleading as though he hadn't even heard it.

For it was only a few months later that Elkalah fell gravely sick. She lingered a week, and then, quite suddenly, closed her eyes and died in the middle of her sleep. She was just thirty years old when Myer heard her voice for the last time.

At first he was too stunned to do anything more than get up in the mornings and sink into bed at night. He walked around in a daze, and sometimes he stumbled into things as though he hadn't watched where he was going. He closed his shop and refused to accept any work, though a number of customers called at his house and asked him when he expected to be doing business. He told them he didn't know, perhaps he was closed for good. He neglected his appearance and people began to think him a little mad, the way he walked around the city with his hair uncombed and half the buttons on his coat undone.

Because of the way he was acting Asher and

his wife, Caty, began to worry about Myer's children. So Caty asked her sister, Joyce Mears, if she would take care of them until Myer got hold of himself and made his own arrangements.

Myer heard all this from Asher and Caty as if in a dream. He nodded and said he would be grateful to her if Joyce Mears came and cooked and took care of his children. But once she was there he rarely looked at her and scarcely knew when she came or left, or even what she was saying.

For now he was concerned with nothing but his own misfortune. It seemed to Myer that his entire universe had been destroyed with the death of Elkalah. There wasn't any point to life itself, as far as he could see. He didn't cry, but sat in his chair in the parlor and stared into the fireplace and asked himself over and over why God had deserted him.

Myer really believed that God *had* deserted him. Otherwise, why had his wife been taken from him so young? What had she ever done to deserve such an early death? And what was the point of it all anyway, the endless work and struggle, when life could end so suddenly, leaving all the best ahead?

God had taken his innocent wife for no reason that he could see. God had taken the wife
of a man who had tried to live by His word.
Myer thought of all he had done for the synagogue and for his fellow Jews who were less
fortunate. He had returned many times over
the money his mother had once received from
the congregation. He had never broken the
Sabbath or God's other Commandments. And
this was his reward. . . .

These were Myer's thoughts as he sat in
front of the fire or went out and wandered
around the city. These same thoughts, over
and over again. . . .

Weeks went by, and Myer's friends and
family grew more and more concerned at his
state of mind. When they tried to talk with
him he would listen and then start to answer,
only to lapse into silence. When they asked
him a question he often didn't seem to hear,
and when he did he would say, "Not now, not
now. I'm thinking. I have certain questions on
my mind. Please don't bother me. I'll discuss
it with you later."

His children grew frightened of him when
they saw how strange he looked and acted.
He seemed like a different person, and they

avoided him and stayed with Joyce Mears as if for protection.

Then Myer gave up going to services and sat home instead, staring out of the window into the empty street. His family worried more each day, but nobody knew what to say to him.

Even though it was the dead of winter, Myer walked the streets almost every day. And one afternoon he looked up to find himself standing in front of Isaac Seixas' fine house. He walked up the steps and hammered on the door. A moment later he found himself with Isaac in the parlor.

Suddenly, without knowing why, all the anger and resentment that he had been harboring against God for taking Elkalah away from him he seemed to feel against Isaac Seixas. He looked at the older man, and said bitterly, "God has deserted me. You're the one who always used to talk so much about God's love and God's mercy. Well, where are they now?"

"They haven't changed," Isaac said.

"Is it a sign of love and mercy to take a man's wife away from him?"

"It may be," Isaac told him. "God doesn't always explain himself to people like us."

"And why not?"

"Because . . . He *is* God. And anyway, what makes you think God has deserted you?"

"He deserted me," Myer said, "when he killed Elkalah. He robbed her of life—and he robbed me of everything *but* life. My whole world's empty now. If God were with me, beside me, the way the psalmist says, would I feel so much alone, would I feel so deserted?"

"Maybe you are alone," Isaac said. "Only maybe it's not God's fault."

"You're talking in riddles," Myer said.

Isaac Seixas, grown older now, looked at Myer sternly. "Maybe," he said, "you feel the way you do because you deserted God—a long time ago. That makes more sense to me than what you're telling me now. After all, how has He deserted you? He's given you four fine children. Any man would be proud of them and happy because of them. He's given you brothers and sisters, nephews and nieces . . . a wonderful family. He's given you success, and a growing reputation as an artist. And now, because he's taken your wife away, you say that God has deserted you. You say you feel alone—well, who drove Him out of your heart if it wasn't you?"

Isaac's face had grown very dark. Now he rose and coming across the room leaned over and pointed his finger at Myer. "You drove God out of your heart a long time ago I think," Isaac said.

"What do you mean?" Myer said angrily. "I've always attended services. I've obeyed the Commandments."

"Of course."

"I've given to charity—more than most. I've taken care of the poor and the sick. What more is required of a man?"

"That he love God with all his heart and all his mind. That he love God more than money and reputation and a fine house on a fine street."

Myer sank back in his chair and said, "How do you know what I love and what I don't? I'm no miser. Who says I love money so much?"

"It's no secret," Isaac said. "I learned some of it from your own brother. And some of it from Elkalah herself. Asher told me about the girl you wanted to marry, but couldn't because you were too poor. It stuck, right inside you, didn't it? So you swore you'd become rich—

and have your revenge on people like that.
That's why you worked so hard, day after day,
year after year, to make more money.

"You worked honorably to get it. And
there's nothing wrong with hard work, or
making money—as long as you don't put it
ahead of everything else. As long as you still
have time for those who love you—like your
wife and children.

"Only some men *do* put wealth ahead of
everything else, Myer. And aren't you really
one of those men? Isn't that why you feel such
emptiness in your heart now? And don't you
know that everything I've been telling you is
true—that when you cry out against God
you're really crying out against yourself?"

Myer felt bitterly angry with Isaac Seixas.
The meddlesome fool! What did he really
know when you got right down to it? It was
easy enough for *him* to preach a sermon about
God and love and all the rest. Isaac was a rich
man, but God didn't take *his* wife away. Easy
to say to someone else, God is merciful, when
God has been merciful to *you*.

"I didn't come here to be lectured," Myer
said. "You don't understand. I don't know

why I ever thought you could." And he rose to his feet and rudely left the room and stormed out of the house.

But at the bottom of his heart Myer knew that Isaac had told the truth. He had worked hard not only because he loved his craft the way all true artists do but also to gain the wealth he had always desired. He had closed his heart to everything else, and since his heart had been filled with nothing but the desire for money, how could God have found room there?

The words of Elkalah finally made him admit this to himself. Her words that haunted him so much now. He could still see her, standing beside their dining room table, saying to him, "We spend so little time together now." And he could hear his own words, as he made another excuse for working late again. "Why, we have all the time in the world together."

And then, as if God had heard and wished to show him the evil that was hidden in his heart, He had taken Elkalah . . . and suddenly there was no time left for them to be together. And the thought of all the years he had wasted made his life bitter. God had given him thirteen years of marriage, and he had spent those years like a profligate. He had wasted so many precious hours. . . . His wife had pleaded with him not to, and he had turned a deaf ear. . . .

Myer suffered remorse for what he had done, but nobody's grief can last forever. In time he began to see that the important thing now was the present and not the past. Gradually his eyes seemed to grow clearer. He looked around and saw what had been happening since Elkalah's death.

He discovered his own children staring at him and starting with fright when he spoke to them. He realized with a pang how little he had said to them for weeks on end. He saw the sign he had hung outside his shop, and he remembered that he still had a family that depended on his labors. And he noticed for the first time Joyce Mears, the woman who had come to his house to care for his children.

One night he thanked Joyce for all her help. He asked her to stay in his house if she would, and continue as a professional housekeeper at a salary. And Joyce, who had no children or a home of her own, agreed to stay if the children wanted her there. Myer asked them, and they all said yes, please let her stay.

Before long Myer opened his shop and went back to work again. But now, no matter how many commissions he still had to finish, he never stayed at his work from dawn till dark. He made it a point to be upstairs in the kitchen when his children were ready for lunch or supper, and he sat down with them and Joyce Mears, and they ate together as a family.

In the evenings he told them stories or went over their lessons with them, because he knew they had no mother now and needed him more than they had ever needed him before.

When Elkalah died Myer had made up his mind that he would never marry again. He was sure that no other woman would ever please him or win his love. Now he went to other people's houses and mingled with their guests. He saw many women in the synagogue and in the street, but none of them seemed able to touch his heart. The pretty ones sometimes reminded him of his dead wife and caused him a stab of pain, but the thought of marrying one of them didn't even enter his mind. Such a marriage would have been a tor-

ture, because their very charms would have reminded him of Elkalah.

Yet he knew, even before people began to
talk to him and hint gently about it, that he
was being unfair to his children. Judith, his
little girl, was almost five years old. She could
scarcely remember her mother now. . . . She
hardly knew what it was to have a mother's
love. And the boys needed more than just a
father's care and companionship.

So, Myer thought to himself, I must marry
one day, for the sake of my children. Only I
don't see how I can. No one could ever take
the place of Elkalah. Yet men do remarry
when they've become widowers. Especially
when they have small children to look out for.

One night he talked of it to his brother,
Asher, and his sister-in-law, Caty. "It isn't
right for a man to stay a widower forever," he
told them. "He must think of his children as
well as himself. I must try to find someone to
marry. . . ."

"Yes, I think you should," Asher said.

"It would be good for all of you, especially
the children, *if* you could find someone," Caty
said.

"But it won't be easy," Myer told them.

"All the same, you need someone for companionship," Caty said. "Everyone does."

Myer nodded, and thought about it as he walked home that night. For companionship . . . that would be the only way. . . .

He opened the door to the parlor and saw Joyce Mears in front of the fireplace. She was sitting just as Elkalah used to sit, with the children gathered around her, their eyes wide with attention, as she read to them by the light of a candle.

"Shouldn't the children be in bed?" Myer said.

Joyce glanced up from the fire, a look of surprise on her face. "Is it so late?" she said.

"Past their bedtime," Myer said. And he watched as she overcame their protests and got them to go upstairs and get ready for sleep.

They seemed to like her very much . . . little Judith to love her as much as if she were her real mother. Joyce was good with his children . . . and they seemed happy when they were with her. . . .

That night Myer's thoughts turned to Joyce for the first time. She had been in his house for almost a year and a half, and he had never thought of her as anything but a kind woman who came there and took care of his children because she had no family of her own.

But what was she really like? Kind, yes, and efficient. Much more efficient than Elkalah had ever been. Joyce ran the household so well that he was never bothered by any of the details. She kept the household accounts, and they were always in order.

Joyce was quite unlike Elkalah, he finally decided. Though they would have been about the same age, Joyce seemed much older and more mature. Before that night it had never occurred to Myer to ask whether Joyce Mears was pretty or not. But now that he thought about it, he was sure that she wasn't. She was just a plain, sensible woman who could manage a household and run things smoothly.

Slowly though, Myer came to change some of his ideas about her. She was plain—but certainly not homely. And he liked her calm manner and her good-natured disposition. He admired the way she took care of the children, too. And when she smiled, though her smile had none of the flashing beauty of Elkalah's, still it was pleasant to see Joyce Mears smile too.

Before many more months went by Myer had decided that Joyce would make him a very good and devoted wife. But he knew that he had to be honest with her. So he said one night, when they were alone in the parlor, "Joyce, you've been here for a long time now. . . . You know me, and the sort of man I am. You know I loved Elkalah—and always will.

"But I don't think she would have wanted me to live alone forever. Especially since my children need a mother to care for them. . . ."

Joyce looked at Myer, but said nothing.

"I'd like you to understand all this—and to be my wife. . . . I'm not a young man any more, and I can't pretend that I love you now the way a young man loves a young girl. But I admire and respect you. . . . You've been kind and loyal to me and my children. . . ."

Joyce Mears's round, pleasant face became creased as she began to cry. Myer never forgot what she said the next moment.

"I'm thirty, Myer . . . thirty years old. . . ." It was said to him as if she were ashamed of being so old and wanted to give him a chance to change his mind.

But Myer didn't want to change it. And he laughed and said, "Well, and how old do you think *I* am? I'm more than forty—so let's not start discussing how old we are."

Myer and Joyce became engaged, and not many weeks later they were married in her father's home. And Judith, Myer's mother, said to him after the wedding, "You're very lucky, Myer. Most men marry only once, and don't always do too well when they do. But you've married twice, and both times you found a prize."

And Myer knew that his mother was right. He had found two lovely and loyal women, Elkalah Cohen, and now Joyce Mears. And his heart slowly was filled with a sense of goodness that he had thought he would never feel again.

He knew that God had given him a second chance for happiness, and he often thought, at prayer and at work, of the words of the 104th Psalm, for the words seemed to say everything that was in his heart. . . .

How manifold are thy works, O Lord!
In wisdom hast thou made them all;
The earth is full of thy creatures. . . .
May the glory of the Lord endure for ever . . .
I will sing unto the Lord as long as I live;
I will sing praise to my God while I have any
    being. . . .

6. *The Shadow of War*

In the years that followed Myer found his marriage to Joyce Mears remarkably peaceful and satisfying. He became a father again. Richea, Moses and Samson were born to him and Joyce, so that in all there were seven growing children in the household.

Although Myer never forgot his first wife,

as time went by Joyce Mears gradually took a place beside her in his love and respect. She was a comfort to him now, and managed her own children and her stepchildren with equal fairness and affection. Her kitchen was always filled with laughter and shouting voices, and sometimes with childish quarrels too. And Myer was often there, settling the quarrels or teasing the children or making up games for them to play.

He still worked hard in the shop below stairs, but he worked with a satisfaction unmixed with any desire to make more money. Only the work itself was important—it had to be beautiful. He didn't care now if he ever became a man of real consequence or not.

Yet he had become one, now that he no longer wished to be any richer than he was or any more important. No silversmith in the city was as highly regarded. The richest men in the colony came to his shop and left their orders. A list of the people he worked for and knew would have contained the names of the most prominent families in early New York.

One day it was a pipe lighter that Myer made for the Cortlands or the Van Rennselaers. Another day it was a pair of candlesticks

for the Livingstons, or a covered mug for the
Appletons, or a pair of coasters for the Schuy-
lers. Many of these pieces may still be seen today, in private collections or in public mu-
seums. And so wide had his reputation grown
that he often received commissions from people in the other colonies; from men like John
Adams in Massachusetts, who commissioned a
silver ladle that is now in the Fogg Museum
in Boston.

The list of his clients was long and impres-
sive, and it pleased Myer that his work should
be so widely recognized and sought. But it
pleased him even more that his skill continued
to grow with the years, and that his work was
now devoted to the creation of beauty for its
own sake, and not for the importance it could
bring him personally.

As the years passed he began to find a new
pleasure in creating religious objects. In 1765
he made a pair of silver scroll bells for the
Congregation Shearith Israel, and an almost
identical pair for the famous Touro Synagogue
in Newport, Rhode Island. The bells' use was
purely ornamental. They were affixed to the
Torah in such a way that as the sacred scroll
was removed from the Ark and carried to the

reading desk, the sound of the bells on top
rang out in the stillness of the synagogue.

Myer was never happier than when he was
making those bells and other ritual ornaments
for his synagogue. It seemed to him the perfect
way for an artist to spend his time, making something beautiful and dedicating that
beauty to his God. It made him feel humble,
for he realized that whatever skill he had been
given, it had come from God, and he himself
in his daily efforts to create beauty was merely
acting out the will of God and shaping the
unformed metal in His name.

Happy with his growing family, happy at
his work, at peace within himself, Myer found
himself thinking that he could wish for nothing more than this: to end his days in such
complete tranquillity. Adventure and excitement? They didn't interest him now. For he
wasn't a young man any more. The year was
1773—and he realized one day, with a jump
of surprise, that he was actually going to celebrate his fiftieth birthday.

He was the oldest member of the family
now. His mother had died that spring, and
here he was, the oldest of her living sons and
daughters. A gray-haired man of fifty, with a

belly that was stout and a face that was lined with soft wrinkles—a far different person from the boy of thirteen who once had sat with his father on a wharf near the East River and talked about the future and what he might become.

That scene on the wharf had taken place almost forty years ago. Now at last he had found contentment, and he didn't want to see anything in his life change. Yet change was going on all around him, and there was nothing that he or anyone else could do to stop it.

The seeds of rebellion were already planted in the colonies; now they seemed almost ready to sprout.

Myer knew and understood the resentment that his neighbors felt toward the English government. Only he wished that somehow an agreement could be reached and tempers smoothed down. Peace. With all his heart he yearned for peace between the colonies and England.

But peace was not to be had, and by 1773 the facts could hardly be escaped if a man was willing to look at them squarely. The colonial troubles had started a decade before with the end of the French and Indian Wars and the defeat of France. A year later the English prime minister, George Grenville, had forced the passage of the Sugar Act through Parliament. According to this law, imports of rum, spirits and molasses from Dutch and French colonies were prohibited.

If observed, the Sugar Act would have bankrupted many of the merchants in New York who were engaged in the West Indian trade. But the law was not followed to the letter. Exceptions were made, and before long the law was openly ignored. Taxes frequently weren't collected. Ships brought in the forbidden articles and didn't even bother to go through the English customs.

The Sugar Act was merely the first of a series of laws passed by England's Parliament that angered the colonies. In the case of the Sugar Act, New York's merchants and shipowners were enraged because their welfare was being sacrificed to the interests of people in England and to people in England's colonies in the West Indies.

The Sugar Act was followed by the Currency Act and the Quartering Act. The first hurt colonial trade even further; the second showed that the colonists' civil rights were at stake. They were forced, at their own expense, to feed and shelter English soldiers in their own homes—whether they chose to or not.

Even more resented was the Stamp Act of 1765, taxing a great many of the goods that the colonials had to buy. Public reaction was strong and immediate. Resolutions were passed by various colonial legislatures; a congress was called in New York, with delegates from nine of the colonies attending; citizens were organized under the name of the "Sons of Liberty," and often mobs of them appeared and attempted to prevent the collection of taxes by the tax officials; pamphlets were circulated; and finally a movement was started to encourage home manufacturers to produce more goods, and to try to keep people from buying British imports.

Feelings in the city and in the colonies grew bitter over other grievances. One of the most angering was a practice called "impressment." Under the Law of Impressment, young Americans could be seized and forced to go aboard ships of the English Navy, to serve on those ships against their will. This practice had long been known and tolerated in England itself, but its appearance in New York and other port cities spread the flames of hatred even further.

Even so, with the Stamp Act's repeal in 1766 affairs grew calmer, and it took a number of years for the spirit of rebellion to mount high in the colonies. Most of the people felt themselves to be loyal British subjects, and they wanted to remain so. They owed allegiance to King George III, but it became more and more clear that neither the king nor his prime ministers understood the position of the colonists or were willing to consider their welfare. England placed her own interests first. Her American colonies would have to make the best of it.

The Townshend Acts, again taxes on various imports, were almost the last straw. They completely ignored the colonists' rights, overruled their protests and showed many uncertain people in the colonies that their trust in the English king was misplaced. If America was ever to have equal status with England it would have to be gained by throwing off the chains of colonial servitude—and the word rebellion was used, though cautiously, for the first time.

Because of the Townshend Acts the colonial cause rapidly grew strong. There were protests of all kinds. The most famous was the "Boston Tea Party," which took place in 1773, when a group of New England citizens refused to pay the import tax and threw 340 tea chests into the harbor.

Still, some of the merchants and tradesmen of New York, like those of Baltimore and Philadelphia, moved their feet slowly. Rebellion had a new, a dangerous, an unwelcome sound. Myer himself felt this sharply. The king had taken away some of their liberties and had harmed their trade, but perhaps he would still relent while there was time.

The debate raged everywhere. In secret places, wherever men met privately, and then at last in public meetings. And there were always men on both sides, men who breathed fire on the one hand and swore that the colonies should declare themselves independent that very hour, and others who said such talk was treason and the speakers should be hanged like thieves in the public square.

In the middle men stood like Myer, looking unhappily on one side and then the other. Men who were against the acts of the king and his prime ministers, but men who couldn't declare for war and bloodshed with an easy mind.

Myer talked about it with Asher and with his wife Joyce and with the various people who came to his shop every day. He talked with the other leaders of the synagogue. His sympathies, he said, were with the new colonial leaders—men like Jefferson and Patrick Henry in Virginia, and like John Adams in Massachusetts. But the course they were taking would almost surely lead to war, and how could anyone counsel war, unless it was the *only* step by which the colonies could secure their rights?

In the following months word of events from the other colonies kept reaching New York. In many of the colonies the legislatures met without consulting the British governor and passed various laws and resolutions to increase their own strength. The men who attended these meetings began to exchange views, drawing the colonies even closer together. By 1774 the First Continental Congress met, with delegates from all the colonies except Georgia. New resolutions were passed urging again the boycott of British goods and encouraging American manufacturers.

Everywhere protests were made against new and repressive laws—against the Quebec Act, against the closing of the port of Boston, against the appointment of General Gage as governor of Massachusetts, with the authority to uphold the new laws by military force.

The spirit of independence was nearly out of control; and then, in the spring of 1775, the battles of Lexington and Concord took place, American militiamen were fighting against British soldiers and almost overnight the War of Independence had begun.

There was no English garrison in New York City, but by January of 1776 it was becoming increasingly clear that the enemy intended to seize the city with his fleet and use it as a major base of operations.

For days now, the Congregation Shearith Israel had been torn in two directions. The Tories among New York's Jews wanted to remain where they were and live under the English if the city was taken. The others, led by a thin, intense young man named Gershom Seixas, wanted to close the synagogue and move themselves and their families to Philadelphia or Connecticut, where they would be free of the British and could aid the colonial cause.

Gershom Seixas was the son of Isaac Seixas. He was the reader, or *Hazzan,* of the synagogue, and his opinion carried great weight among the members of the congregation. But he was opposed by some of the richest members, mostly merchants and traders, led by a man named Barrack Hays.

Both Barrack Hays and Gershom Seixas had come to Myer several times, begging him to take their side. Myer's influence was so strong among the members that with the congregation divided his word would almost certainly decide the question. The synagogue had already made him sole trustee in charge of synagogue property as a mark of their respect and trust. He had only to speak, and the debate would be over.

But Myer found it impossible to speak out. He detested Barrack Hays and the other Tories who wanted to stay in New York and do business with the English. He knew they were men who put profit before patriotism, and he was proud that, though rich and powerful, they were few in number.

But he couldn't find the strength to say to

Gershom Seixas and his followers, "All right, we must leave the city, we must close the synagogue and take our families into danger in order not to help the English in any way."

Myer didn't want to leave the city. He kept hoping, to the very end, that word would suddenly come from England saying that the king had met all the colonists' demands and no war, no bloodshed, no slaughter would be necessary.

The days slipped by, and then one afternoon a message came to Myer from Isaac Seixas. Isaac had been gone from the city for ten years. He had been living in Rhode Island, and Myer hadn't even heard of his return. Could Myer, the message asked, come to Gershom's house? It was very urgent.

Myer put on his hat and coat and set off from his workshop to see Isaac Seixas. Turning the last of several corners, he came to the house and went into the parlor. He saw in front of him a man who was incredibly old. An old man leaning forward, his hands resting for support on the head of a cane. His cheeks were wrinkled and thin. But his eyes were as cool and clear as ever.

They shook hands, and then Isaac Seixas

sat down again. His eyes settled on Myer.
Then he said, "I've been talking to my son
Gershom. He's explained to me the situation
at the synagogue. He tells me the congregation is still waiting for your decision. Well,
Myer—so am I. Shall the Jews of New York
stay here and welcome the English and support their side, or shall they leave and help
in the fight for freedom?"

"You know where I stand," Myer said. "We
must fight the English—if we have to."

"But when are you going to take the final
step?" Isaac said. "When are you going to tell
the congregation that the time to leave the
city is *now?*"

Myer shook his head. "It isn't easy," he said
to Isaac. "I can't tell other men to do what
I'm not willing to do myself. I'm over fifty,
Isaac. At my age shall I lead my family, my
wife and small children, into danger and war?
Well, if I tell others they must do it, then I
must do it myself. But where should we go?
To Pennsylvania or Connecticut? Expose my
children to the open countryside, to the mer-
cies of the Tories and the English? Isaac—it's
a hard choice."

"The choice of freedom is always hard."

"But listen," Myer said. "There's something on the other side too." He sighed and repeated what Barrack Hays had said in the synagogue, though even as he spoke Myer knew he didn't really believe what he was saying. "The English king—he hasn't done any harm to us as Jews. He's hurt us as tradesmen, but no more than anyone else. He may tax us unjustly, deprive us of other freedoms, but he hasn't tried to prevent us from worshipping as we choose. Maybe, when all is said and done, we should stay in New York and try to get along with the English. Sometimes, I'm tempted to think so."

Myer knew all this was a half-truth—but he felt sick and weary at the prospect of leaving his home, taking his family, his small children, and setting off to an unknown place that might be little better than a wilderness.

To answer him, Isaac stood up and went over to the mantelpiece. When he returned, he was carrying a silver object in his hand. At first Myer didn't recognize it in the darkness of the parlor. But slowly he made it out.

Isaac set down the silver Menorah on the table. It was the first Menorah that Myer had ever made, the one that Isaac had ordered at

Wilhelm Skatts's shop when Myer was still an apprentice.

Isaac looked at Myer sharply now. "I've always kept this Menorah with me," he said to Myer, "because, in moments of trial, when I felt I needed strength and courage, the sight of it reminded me of the Maccabees and their fight with their oppressors—and it reminded me of a young apprentice who could stand up and speak the truth in spite of everything.

"But Myer," the old man said, "when the Maccabees fought was it only because they were tired of paying unjust taxes to their overlords? Or was it because, after a time, the temple was desecrated and their right to worship God was denied them?

"You ask me, can we Jews remain in the city with the English, and make our peace with them? You tell me the English king has proved himself tolerant to us Jews. Well, perhaps this one has, but will the next king be so tolerant—or the next one? No, Myer, unless all the citizens of a country are their own masters there is no real freedom for anyone, Jew *or* Christian."

Isaac's hands were shaking as he leaned forward and picked up the Menorah. He held it out and Myer, seeing him do so, took it from his hands.

"I'm giving this back to you," the old man said. "I have no more use for it. My time for courage is over. Keep it. You were a brave young man when you made it. I hope you will prove yourself brave again, now that the congregation needs you. Think of the Maccabees, Myer, our people's bravest fighters, and remember that as long as the land is not free of oppressors—whether they're English, or Roman, or Syrian—the practice of religion, and men's rights in all civil affairs, can never be safeguarded either."

Myer stood up and the old man took him by the hand. "Good-by, Myer. . . ." The old man's eyes were moist as he turned away. "You were almost a son to me . . . don't fail me, and don't fail yourself either. . . ."

Myer returned slowly to his house and set the Menorah on a table. As he looked at it much of his life seemed to flood back, and scenes long forgotten crowded before his eyes. His mother and Asher and his sisters sitting with Isaac Seixas, celebrating Hanukkah. . . . The smith he'd worked for, Wilhelm Skatts, and the way he'd frightened Myer.

. . . Isaac telling Myer's little sisters about the Menorah, about the Maccabees and about their brother and the other kind of courage that men needed too. . . .

Myer picked up the Menorah and examined it on every side. It was still as beautiful as ever, simple in design, completely graceful . . . and after he'd made it he had found his own freedom from Wilhelm Skatts, through the help of Isaac. . . . He had found the courage to tell the truth, even though he was afraid. . . .

That evening a meeting was held at the Congregation Shearith Israel. The synagogue was packed. A rumor had gone out that to-night Myer Myers was to speak out at last.

In the beginning there was a furious and bitter debate. Barrack Hays, short and fat, with smooth gleaming cheeks, began it by saying that the colonists were at least partly wrong in their quarrel with the king. He went on to plead for patience, in the hope that the king would answer their demands in time. And then he said, "And what concern is this quarrel to us Jews anyway? If we leave New York and help the colonial cause we'll lose everything: our shops, our property, perhaps our lives. And for what? For *liberty?* Why, we Jews have all the liberty we need the way things are. What liberty can the colonial government give us that we haven't got already? I say we must remain in New York, and help neither one side nor the other."

There were cheers for Barrack Hays, but not very long or loud ones, and cheers again, mostly from the younger men, after Gershom Seixas had stood up and pleaded with his fellow Jews to leave their homes and go out of the city before the English troops arrived.

There was applause, and then Gershom turned and said, "Our friend and respected brother, Myer Myers has told me that he wishes to say a few words tonight, before we put the matter of leaving the city or remaining here to a final vote. Myer . . ."

Myer stood up, and faced the other members of the congregation. Ordinarily he hated to speak in public, but tonight his mind was so taken up with the question that confronted them all that he had no time to think of his own feelings.

His heart was heavy at first as he faced the congregation. But slowly, as he began to speak, he felt a rising sense of strength come over him.

"My brothers and my friends," he said, "I shall make my speech brief. I have hesitated to speak till now because I had hoped, for months past, that by some kind of miracle, this step could be avoided. But it cannot be. The time is upon us now. We must choose one side or the other in the struggle that's already begun. We must choose either to remain here in our city, and try to make peace with tyranny, or else we must close our homes, say farewell to our beloved synagogue and the city we love so well, and place ourselves finally and forever on the side of liberty.

"For me, the choice is clear. I say we must leave all this behind, that we must join our friends in other cities wherever those friends are; that we must close our homes, and in other places, and in every way that we possibly can, support the Continental Congress, our own free government, against the tyranny of the English crown.

"Within a few days I shall leave the city with my wife and children. As a citizen of this land, and as a Jew, I can do nothing less. In doing this, I am choosing freedom. I hope that there are none of you who tonight will willingly choose slavery."

There were cheers and then a rising babble of voices and finally, when Gershom Seixas managed to bring silence to the synagogue, the question was put to a vote. All those who voted to leave stood on one side. All opposed, on the other. Myer and Gershom Seixas were surrounded by the other members. Barrack Hays and one or two others stood alone.

Myer waited while the members slowly filed out. Then he saw his friend, Gershom Seixas, leave the synagogue. And he saw an old man at Gershom's side. It was Isaac, and the old man was smiling faintly as he tottered along on his cane. For a second his eyes met Myer's. They told Myer that his benefactor and oldest friend was satisfied. And inside his own heart Myer knew that at last he was satisfied too.

7. Exodus

Within a day or two of the debate, the Congregation Shearith Israel had closed the doors of the synagogue. By doing so, the Jews of New York declared firmly and publicly that they had cast their lot with the colonial cause.

Gershom Seixas, the *hazzan* of the congregation, with Myer's help, packed away the sacred scrolls and other property and locked the synagogue for the last time. Once the synagogue was closed a large number of the members left the city and went south to Philadelphia; here they were welcomed by friends and remained for the rest of the war. Like many Jews throughout the colonies, they contributed heavily to the support of Washington's army, and by their gifts of money and goods helped strengthen the new nation in its fight for independence.

Meanwhile, Myer and his family were still in New York, preparing to leave the city for Connecticut. Myer and Asher and a few others had decided to go north to Norwalk, where they had friends and relatives.

It was not easy for Myer to leave his house and workshop behind and set off across the country to a new home. He had never lived anywhere but in New York, and the streets and shops and wharves of the city were very dear to him.

To make things harder he was not an active man, as many of the younger patriots were. He had spent most of his life inside the four walls of his shop, heating and molding the metals of his craft, and his body was not accustomed to the rigors of an active, outdoor life. It was a shock for an older man, a man of fifty-three and the father of a large family, to take up a new and completely different existence.

The day of departure was a trying one for Myer. The train of wagons stood in the street, in front of his house and Asher's. Their belongings were packed in first, then their houses locked, and the children put inside the wagons on top of the bedding and mattresses. Finally Myer helped Joyce into the front and took his place beside her. The reins were in his hands. He looked around—and saw, standing in the street, Barrack Hays and one or two others from the congregation who were Tory sympathizers.

Barrack Hays shook his head sadly and said to Myer, "I'm sorry to see this. You could have stayed here, the way I'm doing, and been perfectly safe. Why endanger your wife and children? For what? The English will beat the rebel army in a month. Why not be sensible, Myer? You still have the chance. Stay. The whole thing will be over soon, and then you can carry on your business as usual."

Myer knew that Barrack Hays didn't want

him or Asher or their friends to stay. He was only taunting them because he thought they'd come crawling back soon, beaten in the war and stripped of their possessions.

Myer smiled down at Barrack Hays. "We'll meet again one day," he said. "And when we do, then you'll have a chance to tell me about your friends, the English." With a signal to Asher and the others to follow, he flicked the horses with the reins and the wagons started away.

They went up the old Post Road, which was the main highway leading out of the city, and before many hours had passed they were traveling through the open countryside, the wagons rocking heavily on the rough country road.

He and Asher had figured to reach Norwalk in three days if they were lucky. But the weather went against them. Rain fell continuously, making it difficult for the horses to haul the wagons. One of the horses threw a shoe and pulled up lame. Their food ran short and they had to ask help at the farmhouses along the way. Although they had money and offered to pay, several of the farmers, because they secretly favored the English, refused them food and turned Myer and Asher away empty-handed.

Asher, who had always been the easygoing one, exploded when he heard what the farmers said. But Myer, grown older and wiser now, calmed him down.

"What's the use of complaining?" he said to his brother. "These people are afraid, just like Barrack Hays was. Afraid for their own skins. That's why they favor the English. And that's why they're afraid to help us by selling us food, even though they see how desperate we are."

"Of course we're desperate," Asher said. "We have more than a dozen children to feed . . ."

"We'll try the next farmhouse," Myer said. "All the people here can't be Tories. We'll find food soon."

Another turn in the road, another farmhouse, and this time a friendly greeting, with food and a place by the roaring fire. And afterward Myer and Asher and their wives and children gave thanks with prayer for the friendliness they had finally met with on their flight from the city.

Then they took to the road again, with fresh supplies that they'd bought, and their horses rested and newly shod. The weather cleared, and the wagons rolled slowly along the rutted roads until at last, two days later, they made their way into Norwalk.

Here friends greeted them and took them into their homes. They helped the new settlers, and before long Myer and Asher and the other refugees were all living in new quarters.

Myer and Asher had brought their tools with them. They each went to work building a workshop while their wives arranged their new rooms as comfortably as they could.

In the spring of the year another child, Rebecca, was born to Myer and Joyce. Myer was working as a silversmith again, to earn money for his family, but he found his time taken up more and more with patriotic affairs.

In July news reached the refugees in Norwalk that the English had landed on Long Island. There were battles with Washington's troops, and Washington's army was defeated. More bad news followed. Washington was said to have retreated to the city, pursued by the British. He retreated again, north this time, won a skirmish on Morningside Heights, but then retired to New Jersey in the face of a larger enemy force. New York was now entirely in English hands.

In Norwalk, as elsewhere, there was discouraging talk. One day Myer overheard a New Haven merchant named Isaacs speaking against the colonial troops under Washington. Myer felt his temper rise. He was tempted to strike the other man—but then his calmer side prevailed. He and a friend of his, who had heard Isaacs' talk, signed a charge against the merchant to try and have him punished for spreading such stories. The court records fail to indicate whether Isaacs was convicted or not, but after that Myer became even more convinced that the new nation's cause was in peril if American citizens thought so little of their own government and its soldiers— and he vowed to do all that he could to help the colonial cause at every opportunity.

Although the coast of Connecticut still remained in colonial hands, the English soon began to raid coastal towns like New Haven and Norwalk, sending ships of their fleet up Long Island Sound to strike against the defenseless residents.

In 1778 and again in 1779 raiders sailed

into Norwalk and burned and robbed everywhere. The second time Myer awoke in the middle of the night to see strange, flickering lights dancing on the walls of his bedroom. He leaped out of bed and dashed to the window. Not far away he saw a house already in flames, the occupants running down the street in their nightclothes. The English raiders had landed and were sacking the place—there was no time to lose.

Myer woke the children up. Then, carrying the youngest in his arms, he and Joyce and the older children were forced to flee. Taking what possessions they could, they ran out of their house and away from the approaching flames.

They found shelter that night with friends, and in the morning, when Myer returned to his house, he found it looted and ransacked and half of it burned out by the fire that the soldiers had started deliberately.

Asher's house and several others suffered a similar fate. He and Myer lost many of their tools, their household articles and most of their furniture. Without proper tools it would be harder for them to earn money for their families, and they had to buy new furnishings to replace what the English had stolen or destroyed.

As he looked at the charred shell of his house, Myer shook his head and asked himself with discouragement how much suffering a man was expected to endure in this world. He had a family to feed and clothe and shelter. He had already given a great deal of money to support the militia. Now he had lost many of his dearest possessions. Joyce, he saw, was trying to hold back her tears as she looked at her household prizes, burned or broken or torn to shreds.

And then Myer remembered why they were there, standing in a strange town, looking at a ruined house. They were there for the same reason that his parents, Solomon and Judith Myers, had come to America more than half a century before—to find liberty and justice for themselves and their children in a world where liberty and justice were hard to find.

Among the ruins of their house Myer and Joyce discovered the Menorah that Isaac Seixas had returned to him. And Myer thought to himself, there's no point in complaining. The Maccabees didn't when they were fighting in the mountains against their Syrian oppressors. And all of us are Maccabees now, even our little children.

He looked at the Menorah and decided that he would keep it nearby wherever he went during the rest of the war. In case, he thought, my courage fails me. Then I will see it and be able to get control of myself again. I must keep it close by, no matter where I am. For if this is the sort of thing that the English do, if this is the kind of people they are, then we must all try that much harder to aid our country in her fight against them.

But what else could a man like Myer do except to contribute money to the colonial government? He thought for a long time, seeking the answer. And whenever an opportunity to help presented itself, he always accepted it willingly.

First, he joined his fellow citizens in petitioning the Connecticut authorities for a ship to patrol Long Island Sound and protect them against future raids by the English fleet. He signed a petition to reduce the taxes of those among his neighbors who had been left destitute by the raids. But all this was not enough. Myer hunted through his mind—and one day remembered a letter that had come to him almost five years before.

The letter had asked him then if he would consider melting down lead to make bullets for the government. Now Myer remembered what he had been hearing lately about the desperate shortage of lead bullets among the soldiers.

As soon as his family found better quarters Myer took out his wagon and started around the countryside. He stopped at any house he saw and offered to buy the lead strips from the windows, and any other lead they had. More often than not when the owners learned why Myer wanted the lead they allowed him to take it away for nothing. Then he put the strips of lead into his wagon and drove back home, where he melted the lead down in his workshop and molded it into bullets.

Finally, with the help of Joyce and the children, he packed the bullets into boxes and carried the boxes to the wagon. He put the boxes on the bottom and covered them over with straw and a collection of farm implements.

Then, dressed in rough country clothes

and trying to look as much like a country peddler as he could, he prepared to deliver the bullets to the American soldiers.

Before he left, he and Joyce and the children said a prayer and asked God to protect him on the journey. For the roads that he had to take were patrolled by English cavalry and if the bullets were discovered under the straw in his wagon, then Myer would have been arrested and imprisoned, and perhaps even hung as a traitor.

So they prayed together for God's mercy and protection, and then Myer went outside to the wagon. Joyce and the children came too, and one of the smaller children gave him the Menorah. Myer took it, and while the children watched, tucked it into the back of the wagon, under the straw.

"As long as I have it with me," Myer said, "I have the spirit of the Maccabees with me too." Then he climbed up on the wagon, picked up the reins and gave them a flick. The horses started, and Myer rolled away on his dangerous journey.

Often when he was out like this he had to drive twenty or thirty miles before reaching a place where he could safely deliver the bullets. Most of the time his heart beat hard enough, but it seemed to jump right into his throat whenever he caught sight of an English patrol and the soldiers with their long swords and their scarlet uniforms.

The first two times he was stopped by a patrol he was allowed to pass by without any real trouble. But the third time he was not so lucky.

"You say you're a peddler?" the young officer in command of the patrol asked Myer suspiciously.

Myer nodded his head.

"Well, if you're a peddler, what do you deal in?"

"Almost everything, but farm implements mainly," Myer said.

The officer made Myer dismount, and then he began to look into the back of the wagon. He glanced at the implements that Myer had put on top of the straw. Then he grunted, and his round red face appeared satisfied.

All at once he turned, and glared at Myer. "What's under the straw in your wagon?" he bellowed.

Myer didn't hesitate. "What makes you think there's *anything* there?" he said.

"Because the wagon looks heavy. What are you carrying under the straw?"

Myer drew up close to the officer. Suddenly —he winked.

"It's a sideline with me," Myer said, as if he were giving away a great secret. "I sell religious objects to the Jews along the coast. There's some money to be made in that sort of thing. The objects are made of metal, brass or silver—that's why my carriage looks so heavy."

"Religious objects?" the officer said, more suspicious than ever. "What kind? Show me, and be quick about it!"

Myer's hand reached under the straw and, with a silent prayer that one would be enough to satisfy the officer's suspicions, he pulled out the Menorah that he always carried with him in his wagon.

"It looks like the real thing," the officer said. "I've seen these Jewish candleholders before myself." Then his eyes grew crafty again. "Only why under the straw?" he said.

"Well, some people aren't very broad-minded," Myer said quickly. "They don't always like to deal with a merchant who sells things like this to the Jews. But these are hard times. I have to sell where I can, to *whoever* I can. So I sell to the Jews, and then I hide their things when I sell my farm implements to the farmers around here. And what the farmers don't know can't hurt them," Myer added with another wink. "Don't you agree?"

The officer grunted a second time and nodded his head. "All right," he finally said. "I don't see anything wrong. You can pass on."

Myer climbed back on the front seat and with a word to his horse rode off with his cargo of bullets. Not till he was out of sight did he stop to wipe the cold sweat from under his hatband and to thank his Maker that he had thought of the Menorah in time to figure out a plausible story.

But this adventure convinced Myer's friends that it was no longer anything but foolhardy for him to continue to deliver bullets through the enemy lines this way. His friends suspected that Tory sympathizers in Norwalk knew what he was doing, and that they had told the English of their suspicions. Next time, his friends said, Myer would be caught and put in prison, and perhaps hung.

It wasn't even safe for him and his family

to stay where they were in Norwalk. The British might raid the town again, and if they did they could still take him prisoner on suspicion of helping the colonial troops. And even if they didn't imprison him, life in Norwalk would never be free of danger. A raid could be expected at almost any time, with more burning and pillaging and destruction of property and lives.

Rather than see his home in flames again and his family forced to flee in the dead of night, Myer decided to take the advice of his friends and leave Norwalk for Philadelphia. There the colonial cause was secure and there was no threat of enemy attack.

So once again he and Joyce packed their belongings on their wagon, and with Asher and his family, they left Norwalk behind and set out for the south.

The journey was even more difficult than their flight from New York. To reach Philadelphia they had to travel by a roundabout route avoiding New York, where the English remained in power. The roads were often impassable because of the rain and mud, and much of their bedding and clothes became soaked with water. The two youngest children, Rebecca and little Benjamin, who had been born in Norwalk, caught a fever, and for days they hovered between life and death.

But at last an end came to the nightmare. Their prayers were answered and the children began to recover from the fever. The family traveled south again, through the level farmlands of New Jersey, where the horses were able to haul the wagons along at a better pace. In time the journey was behind them, and around another turn in the road they came on a welcome sight—the distant outline of the city itself.

Myer and his family were treated with great kindness in Philadelphia. They quickly found a home to settle in and were surrounded by friends and admirers. Myer's reputation as a silversmith was well known in the city. He had made scroll bells and other ceremonial objects for the Congregation Mikveh Israel more than a dozen years before. He had made numerous bowls and plates and other ornaments for various Philadelphia citizens. Now his old customers called at his shop to welcome him. Many placed new orders, so that he was able to buy and furnish his new home and recover his losses.

Myer was also admired in all quarters of the city for his aid to the patriotic cause. In particular he was honored by his fellow congregationists from New York. They remembered the debate in their synagogue, and how Myer had helped them choose freedom instead of servitude. For by now the acts of the enemy had convinced them that the English *were* tyrants. The Declaration of Independence convinced them that the new nation they were helping to build was going to give freedom to all people, no matter what their faith.

The Jews of New York, in their exile, like the Jews in all the colonies, were proud that a new nation was being born such as the world had never seen before. And because of Myer and Gershom Seixas, the Jews of New York had supported that nation in its most critical hour. Now they could be proud of the choice they had made five long years before.

There had been news that their synagogue in New York was being used as a troop barracks and that the sacred objects had been profaned by the soldiers. And the people said to Myer, "Well, and what do you suppose Barrack Hays has been doing in New York lately? How do you imagine he likes it when

his English friends use our synagogue to quar-
ter their troops?"

They shook their heads, and so did Myer,
because it was a bitter thing to think of their
synagogue in enemy hands.

Gershom Seixas, who was in Philadelphia
too, often came to visit Myer, and they ex-
changed stories of what they had done in the
years since they had parted in New York.
Then they began to talk about the future,
and especially about their return to the city
once the war was over. Gershom didn't think
it would be very long. The tide of battle had
begun to run against the English, particu-
larly after the French had come into the war
against them.

"Another year or two and the English will
be beaten," Gershom said one night. "That's
what people are saying. And then we'll be
able to return to our homes."

The rumors proved to be correct. Less than
a year later the English commander surren-
dered at Yorktown, and the final battle of the
American Revolution was over. Two more
years were needed to negotiate the peace; then,
in New York, in November 1783, the English forces evacuated the city and Myer and

the other Jewish exiles prepared to return.

He and his family arrived in early December and hurried down the familiar streets. Their house had been occupied by enemy soldiers and was heavily scarred and damaged. But Myer and Joyce were used to finding scarred furniture and ruined stores. They fell to work setting things to rights and were thankful the damage hadn't been worse.

It was wonderful just to be home again after eight years of living in strange places. To be back in New York, with the war over and freedom won. Myer said it was a perfect present for his sixtieth birthday.

And he laughed and gathered his wife and children around him, and he said to them, "God is truly merciful, and truly wonderful to those He loves. He forced us to go into the wilderness, just like our ancestors. To seek a land of freedom, just as they did. And after many trials we found that land—only in our case it was right here where we started from.

"And we can tell that God has favored us, for how else could a people almost totally unarmed have battled and won freedom from their armed enemies? Even the Maccabees

couldn't do that. . . . So this time God has
helped us with a greater miracle."

Myer could hardly wait to see the rest of
the city again, and the familiar places that
meant so much to him. But one of the first
things that he saw didn't please him. That
was the sight of Barrack Hays and a small
group of Jewish Tories slipping quickly onto
one of the ships to avoid meeting any of the
returning Jews from Philadelphia. Sentiment
was high against the Tories, and Barrack
Hays and the others left while they could, and
never returned again.

It should have been a moment of triumph
for Myer, but he no longer felt any bitterness
toward men like Barrack Hays. He considered
himself fortunate—his family safe, his home
safe—the future secure at last. Secure, not only
for himself and his wife, but for their children
and their grandchildren, for any Jews who
would come to America and swear their allegiance to the new nation.

He remembered his mother and father, the
dangers they'd faced and the uncertainty in
coming to the New World. They had been
right, Myer realized. And all their descend-
ants, he and Asher and all the rest, would al-

ways be grateful for the wisdom of Solomon and Judith.

Their parents had sought liberty more than fifty years before. And now, at last, liberty had finally come to a land called America.

8. The Last Days

The price that Myer had to pay for the years in exile was ill-health and restricted activity. Months of exposure to all kinds of weather had their effect. His chest was weak. The doctor said he was like his father in that respect. He would have to take care of himself from now on. He developed a chronic cough that grew worse at night, or when he tried to do too much and tired himself.

But a little thing like a cough couldn't rob him of the pleasure of being home again. He talked to old friends, in the old places. He opened his shop for business. And because he was known everywhere as one of America's first great artists, he always had more commissions than he could accept. He passed many of them along to other less well-established craftsmen. To protect his health, he worked only half a day, very often on objects for the Congregation Shearith Israel, or for congregations in other states.

With more leisure now, Myer continued his interest in public affairs. When, in 1784, a committee of three was formed by the congregation to greet Governor George Clinton, former leader of the state's militia, Myer was elected one of the members.

He presented a letter to the governor, stating that it came from the Jewish people of the city, many of whom had just returned from exile.

His fellow Jews, Myer said, had abandoned their homes and had gone to Pennsylvania and Connecticut, there to oppose the English

in any way that they could. Now, returning to
their own city, they took this opportunity of
welcoming the governor and of reminding
him, in the light of their patriotic service, of
the need for continuing the rights already
established in New York for all citizens—the
rights of free speech, assembly and public
worship.

Governor Clinton recognized Myer and, to
Myer's surprise, said that he and his wife still
had a set of table silver, made by Myer almost
fifteen years before. "The finest I've ever
seen," the governor said.

Myer bowed. And the governor said, "The
message from your people is well put. Freedom of religion will be maintained here. I've
heard of what various Jewish people from
New York, plain people and leaders like yourself, did during the war. Neither the State of
New York, nor the thirteen United States will
ever forget those deeds. Tell that to your congregation. Their right to worship God as they
choose will never be disputed here."

They shook hands again, and after a few
more words Myer left the governor's presence.
He left with the certainty that he had taken
the right course in the debate with Barrack

Hays, and that he had induced his fellow Jews to act wisely so many years before. The tyranny of a king could never have guaranteed the Jewish people their freedom. A democracy, the kind that was growing in America, could.

The first presidential inauguration also took place in New York, not far from where Myer and Joyce still lived with their youngest children. They both went to what is now the corner of Broad and Wall Streets and joining the throng there, waited as President Washington appeared on the second floor of the Federal Building. Washington made his address and Myer and Joyce, hearing his words, knew that their years of hardship and struggle and flight had not been in vain.

Later, at a public reception, they met the president. Myer felt a sense of awe, almost the same as he had felt as a young man in the presence of Isaac Seixas. Such men carry with them a sense of greatness, a simplicity mixed with confidence that they are capable of performing whatever tasks fate may ask of them. Myer felt awe, and afterward told Joyce, "I never saw a man like that before. You felt like looking up to him. He's the only man I ever met that people must naturally respect."

Joyce smiled to herself—she had heard the same thing said several times in the last few years about Myer himself; but she knew if she told him so he wouldn't have believed her. The more important he had become in the eyes of other men the less her husband seemed aware of it, and the less he cared for marks of public favor.

"Today I met a great man," Myer said. "It was the finest day in my life. That was the way I felt, talking to the president of our country. . . ."

Then gradually the excitement died away in the city and life returned to normal. Myer was a contented man. Joyce had given him six children. Through the years she had remained a devoted wife, bringing him comfort and ease as he grew older. The children he had had by Elkalah were married, so now he had grandchildren surrounding him too.

He spent many hours with them, visiting their different homes and bringing them presents and sitting around the open fireplace, telling stories in the evenings.

At Hanukkah he liked to invite his grand-children to supper. He always lit the candles, and then, pointing to the silver Menorah, would tell them the story of the Maccabees, and the story of the Menorah itself. Of his own struggles with Wilhelm Skatts, and how Isaac Seixas, the father of their own synagogue reader, Gershom, had helped him when he had been a young apprentice.

During the peaceful years that followed the war Myer also liked to walk around New York, the city that he had known and loved for such a long time. Sometimes he and Joyce would leave their house and, walking arm in arm, would spend the afternoon gazing at the shops and houses and wharves and other points of interest in the city.

New York itself had grown much larger. It was still growing. Walking north, Myer would point to a row of houses, and then with a laugh would say to Joyce, "Now here was the stockade we built in 1746 . . . when I was a young man of twenty-three. You can't remember that, I suppose?"

"Can't remember it?" Joyce said. "Why I was eight or nine then—the stockade was built to keep out the Indians."

"Imagine . . . to keep out the Indians," Myer said, looking now at the new houses that stretched so far, where a few years before there had been only open fields.

Many of the places where he and Asher had played as boys had disappeared as well. The meadows, the fresh country streams, the stretches of woodland, all had been turned into streets and houses and shops with smoking chimney pots and brass door handles shining in front. New York had grown up right under his eyes without his noticing it. It had changed from a small, bustling seaport town into a commercial city bursting with new energy.

Of course it was still a seaport, and would always remain so. Sometimes, alone or with Joyce, Myer walked the few dozen yards to the old docks and, standing on the wooden planks, would look out at the water and the shores of Long Island and remember how often he had visited these same docks as a boy.

He remembered more than once the day he had come there with his father and they had sat on an old crate in the warm sunlight and talked of the future. What did Myer want to be? He could almost hear his father, Solomon, asking him to think about it. . . .

And seeing the sailors now (how little the sailors had changed, with their loud voices, their swaggering gait, the coins jingling in their pockets), seeing them on the docks, Myer remembered that day so long ago when he had actually believed he wanted to become a sailor. . . .

"You, a sailor?" he could hear his mother say. And he remembered his childhood seasickness, the time he and some friends had tried to sail a raft across to the opposite shore.

He had wanted to be a sailor, and a blacksmith, and finally a silversmith. Mr. Van Dyck's shop, where he had first seen polished silverware, was gone now, but whenever Myer passed down the narrow street he remembered the day when he had been running an errand for one of his father's customers and had stumbled into another world. A world of beauty that he had never dreamed of before. He remembered the moment when he'd opened the door of the shop and heard the bell tinkle above his head, and discovered the beauty that was to fill his own life for so many years afterward. What a fortunate chance that had been. How lucky he had been in almost every respect throughout his life.

Sometimes, when he looked back on the past, Myer wondered how he could ever have thought that God had deserted him. He remembered the way he had complained to Isaac Seixas that he was deserted, and how wrong he'd been to complain. And other things filled his mind when he counted his blessings. The memory of Elkalah, his first wife, had grown dim, but sweeter if anything. In all of their children he seemed to see her face, and in their voices to hear her voice.

"God has given you children," Isaac Seixas had said to him—and he realized with a sad smile that Isaac had said those words more than thirty years before.

In his walks around the city Myer sometimes turned in the other direction, and instead of inspecting the wharves and docks went south to the tip of the island. Here was the old fort, once the residence of the English governor.

He and Asher had stood there so many times as boys, watching the English soldiers on parade. Now, from one end of the city to the other, there wasn't an English soldier to be seen. Myer couldn't help but smile at the thought of *that* change.

The English were gone forever. And all the years in Connecticut, the night when he and Joyce had been driven from their home with their children clustered about them, the day he had almost been caught with a wagonload of bullets for the American soldiers, the risks and the hardships, all had been worth the price paid.

He found with each passing year that even the cruelest memories seemed to fade away. It was harder and harder for him to understand the excitement and ill will that the younger people felt among themselves—he had to make an effort to remember that he himself had been like that too, if not a good deal worse. Myer and his quick temper. . . . Myer and his bitterness over the girl who wouldn't marry him because he was too poor. . . . The way he had let one disappointment almost poison his life—how strange and far away all that seemed now.

And he would look at the fort for a moment or two longer and then, drawing his coat around him a little closer to keep out the chill, would walk slowly back to his home and his fire, an old man with a stout waist and thin legs, leaning on a cane.

He was careful of his chest because of the cough he had first picked up during the war. Sometimes he wore a muffler knitted by Joyce or one of his daughters to keep the cold out of his throat. He usually remembered to wear one, but sometimes he grew forgetful, as he did on a cold December morning in the year 1795. He was halfway to the synagogue for the early Sabbath Service when he remembered it and didn't bother to return to the house to get it.

He felt a chill by the time he reached the synagogue, but the feeling soon passed away. The service seemed especially beautiful that day. It pleased Myer to see how well the scroll bells kept their brightness, and how much their presence, when the Ark was open, added to the sacred moment . . . and he was glad to have been given the talent to create such loveliness in God's glory, and the chance to use that talent for so many years. . . .

People said afterward that they saw Myer Myers that day making his way slowly home. They remembered that snow had begun to fall, and that an icy wind burst down the streets. They said they nodded to Myer, and that he smiled and nodded in return. A man and his wife had walked with him the few steps to his home, and had said good day to him in the street.

They were the last people to see Myer outside his house. That night he went to bed early, complaining of pains in his chest. He was already suffering a fever. Before long it proved too much for his weakened body, and by another day and evening he had closed his eyes and, without a word, died with complete peacefulness.

He was laid to rest in the same cemetery where his mother and father and his first wife, Elkalah, were buried, in the little cemetery near Chatham Square. It was a sunny day, though traces of snow still clung to the ground and along the rooftops. A cold, clear day, with his family and friends gathered there, and with Gershom Seixas to read the service.

The service was a simple one. Gershom said that Myer would have preferred it that way. "He became more humble, the longer he lived," Gershom said. "We shall never forget

him, for the great artist he was, the patriotic
citizen and the kind friend.

"As a friend he was loyal and devoted. As an
artist he was interested only in the beautiful.
And as a patriot he was an inspiration to us all,
an example. Many of us who left New York for
the sake of our beliefs were young men. Myer
Myers was over fifty. The choice was hard for
him—but he made it without flinching. The
world may remember Myer Myers for the great
artist he was—but if the world has a true
memory it will also remember him for the
deeds he performed for his country . . . the
country he loved so well. . . ."

And then Gershom said, "I would like to
read my friend Myer Myers' favorite psalm,
because I think it expresses the peace he found
at the end of his life . . . after so many struggles with the world, and with himself. . . ."

And in the little cemetery off Chatham
Square Gershom Seixas read aloud the Twenty-
third Psalm while the sun shone down on the
people attending and on the snowy rooftops
and the bare winter ground. And the words of
the psalm told them of God's love—the love

to which Myer Myers finally returned when he was no longer a young man, the love that can reach and enfold all men, wherever they live, and whoever they are.

Covenant Books

Stories of Jewish Men and Women To Inspire and Instruct Young People